WADSWORTH PH

ON

GANDHI

Bart Gruzalski
Pacific Center for Sustainable Living

WADSWORTH

THOMSON LEARNING

Australia • Canada • Mexico • Singapore • Spain
United Kingdom • United States

Printed in the United States of America
2 3 4 5 6 7 04 03 02 01

For permission to use material from this text, contact us:
Web: http://www.thomsonrights.com
Fax: 1-800-730-2215
Phone: 1-800-730-2214

For more information, contact:
Wadsworth/Thomson Learning, Inc.
10 Davis Drive
Belmont, CA 94002-3098
USA
http://www.wadsworth.com

ISBN: 0-534-58374-1

Contents

Preface

Gandhi was one of the most remarkable persons of the twentieth century. Part of what makes him remarkable is that he lead a successful non-violent revolution to free India from British colonial rule. But even more important is his enduring legacy of practical ideas that are relevant to the problems we face today.

In this book we will explore Gandhi's views on non-violence as a technique of social transformation, as a constitutive element of a society, and as an integral part of an individual's way of life. Gandhi's account of non-violence is undoubtedly his best-known legacy. I will argue that it has been too quickly dismissed by those who write about justifications of violence. We will also explore Gandhi's criticisms of globalization and his constructive proposals for decentralized economies, appropriate technology, and self-reliant communities. Finally, we will explore Gandhi's emphasis on, and account of, inner work, which has been a casualty of contemporary academic orthodoxy.

Gandhi believed that the implementation of his proposals would lead to a society free from the problems of violence, unemployment, poverty, and exploitation. Since ecological concerns are now headline news, I also take these into consideration in assessing Gandhi's proposals. In particular, I will ask whether Gandhi's proposals might mitigate the looming ecological crises that we face and that endanger future generations. In discussing these topics I try to present Gandhi's views as fully and accurately as possible in light of current developments and discussions in economics, sociology, and environmental science. What we find, I believe, is that Gandhi was ahead of his time. He not only foresaw many of the problems we face today, but he developed practical proposals to solve them.

Source Material

Gandhi's collected works are ninety volumes, although there is material by him that is not found in these volumes. For the person initially discovering Gandhi, I recommend the classic biography of Gandhi by Louis Fisher, *Gandhi: His Life and Message for the World*, as well as the 1982 movie "Gandhi." Although there are many texts on Gandhi, the best resource for understanding Gandhi is his own writings. Gandhi's autobiography, *The Story of My Experiments With Truth*, is a good place to begin, as is the anthology edited by Louis Fisher, *The Essential Gandhi: His Life, Work and Ideas* (1962). In addition, I recommend *The Mind of Mahatma Gandhi* (edited by R.K. Prabhu and U.R. Rao, 1967) and the three-volume anthology *The Moral and Political Writings of Mahatma Gandhi* (edited by Raghavan Iyer, 1987).

Citations

I cite three works throughout this book. The first is Gandhi's collected works. I refer to this collection as 'CW' and cite the volume and page number. The first citation in this book to the Collected Works is to Volume 62, page 224 and appears in the text as: "(CW 62, 224)." Passages in Gandhi's autobiography, *The Story of My Experiments with Truth*, are all in the *Collected Works*. However, since this single-volume autobiography is much more accessible to readers than the ninety-volume *Collected Works*, I cite the autobiography (as "A") whenever I am referring to a passage from it. Since there are several editions of the autobiography available to the reader, I cite passages by part and chapter number. My first citation is to the autobiography, Part I, chapter xviii and appears in the text as: "(A I, xviii)." I also occasionally cite *The Mind of Mahatma Gandhi* and cite the page number. The first citation to this work is to page 144 and appears in the text as: "(M, 144)."

Abbreviations

CW   *Collected Works*

A   *My Experiments with Truth*

M   *The Mind of Mahatma Gandhi*

Acknowledgments

A number of colleagues and friends reviewed the entire manuscript and I am very grateful to them for their contributions. David Lyons made extensive comments that not only led to significant improvements in the text, but our extended discussion helped me to clarify, at least in my own thinking, key points and their interconnections. V.V. Raman and Ron McAllister sent comments that also prompted significant improvements. Conversations with Jon Boone and with Robie Tenorio, as well as written comments from each, helped me further to improve the text. Chuck Yannacone provided written comments that helped me make the book better, searched out some hard-to-find Gandhi material, and hosted me during two research trips to the University of California at Davis. Kitty Chen contributed her editorial expertise and the final product is remarkably improved for her generous assistance.

Several people made contributions to individual chapters and I want to thank each of them. Paul Encimer helped me to improve significantly the chapter on Gandhi's challenge to the contemporary paradigm of violence. Henry West helped with an early version of key arguments in that chapter. Gillian Brown, Kathy Epling, and Bob McKee each made helpful comments on various chapters. Arvind Sharma informed me of incidents from Gandhi's life and the *satyagraha* struggle that were relevant to the book, although I was able to include only one. David Katz not only raised a key question that led to an important revision of the chapter on assessing Gandhi's blueprint, but, during a prolonged period of computer malfunctions, generously gave of his time and expertise, and provided some critical parts, to keep the project going.

I very gratefully acknowledge my spouse, Marion Gruzalski, who read several versions, discussed Gandhi with me over the years, and supported this project as only a life partner can.

I want to express my deepest appreciation to Daniel Kolak, the editor of this series, for inviting me to write this book on Gandhi's thought. His invitation, comments, and encouragement have not only resulted in this text, but have motivated me to try to understand accurately both the depth and the relevance of one of the great practical thinkers of the twentieth century.

I am very thankful to all of these persons for their various contributions. The book is better for their efforts. I take full responsibility for whatever errors, confusions, misconceptions, or gaps remain.

Several people have encouraged my work on Gandhi over the years. S.S. Rama Rao Pappu invited me to his university as a Gandhian lecturer and has, on many occasions, invited me onto various programs to present material on Gandhi. I am deeply grateful to him for his encouragement and support and for an early discussion of the themes developed in this book. I am also deeply grateful for the encouragement and support of Deen Chatterjee and K. R. Sundararajan, each of whom has also invited me to his respective university to lecture on Gandhi.

A few people played key roles in my early study of Gandhi. Geshe Michael Roach suggested I end a course on Buddhism and Hinduism with a section on Gandhi, and that was an important start. Newton Garver invited me to comment on a paper by Virginia Held, and that was my first attempt to respond to the orthodox objection to Gandhi's non-violence. Shivesh Thakur, Jack Weir, and Barry Gan each enouraged me to write about Gandhi, or Gandhi-related topics, for various publications. I gratefully acknowledge each of these persons for playing an instrumental role in my learning more about Gandhi's thought.

Some material in this book has appeared earlier. I thank *Philosophy in the Contemporary World* for letting me use parts of "Healing Contemporary Problems of Unemployment, Societal Breakdown, and Ecological Degradation: Gandhi's Vision of a Sustainable Society" (Fall, 1994). I also thank Barry Gan, editor of *The Acorn*, for allowing me to use material from my "Gandhi's Challenge To Our Paradigm of Justifiable Violence" (Spring, 2000).

Finally, I thank John Haring who provided a working computer and printer at a crucial moment when a glitch in the solar power system left me without adequate electricity.

1

An Ordinary Beginning

Mohandas Karamchand Gandhi was born on October 2, 1869, at Porbunder, Kathiawar, India. The youngest of three sons, there was nothing especially remarkable about him. His parents betrothed him to Kasturba when he was seven, and they were married when he was thirteen.

After he finished school in India, Gandhi sailed to London to study law. Like young people everywhere he tried to fit the model of the kind of person he thought he was supposed to be, and so he dressed stylishly and even sported a mustache for a time. Underneath the stylish dress was a young man struggling with insecurities and personal shortcomings. One that plagued Gandhi in London was his inability to speak in public. At a meeting of the Committee of the Vegetarian Society he did not feel able to read the short speech he had written in defense of one of the members and someone else read it for him. "Even when I paid a social call," he wrote, "the presence of half a dozen or more people would strike me dumb." (A I, xviii) At another vegetarian meeting he rose to give his speech but failed completely. Although the speech was quite short, "my vision became blurred and I trembled." (A I, xviii) After he passed his examinations, he arranged a farewell vegetarian dinner party in a well-known London restaurant the day before returning to India. At the gathering there would be speeches and he planned to make his

1

humorous. When his turn came, he stood up and began with a joke. After telling the joke, his mind went blank. "My memory entirely failed me," he wrote, "and in attempting a humorous speech I made myself ridiculous." (A I, xviii) Gandhi's inability to speak in public plagued him after he was back in India. In his first legal case, his debut in the court, he stood to cross-examine the plaintiff's witness. Gandhi recalled:

> I stood up, but my heart sank into my boots. My head was reeling and I felt as though the whole court was doing likewise. I could think of no question to ask. The judge must have laughed.... But I was past seeing anything. I sat down and told the agent [his client] that I could not conduct the case. (A II, iii)

His law practice in India fizzled out and he was offered an opportunity to take on some legal work for a firm in South Africa. In South Africa he experienced, for the first time, the racism that Indians in South Africa suffered as part of their daily life. In a meeting that touched on the conditions of Indians in South Africa, he gave his first public speech. Gandhi does not tell us what made this attempt successful, but it was the first of many and he had overcome a debilitating personal shortcoming.

After working for almost a year on the case for which he had gone to South Africa, Gandhi came to see that neither his client nor his client's opponent would financially survive the mounting legal costs. Gandhi "strained every nerve to bring about a compromise." He persuaded both parties to accept arbitration. After his client prevailed, he persuaded him to allow the defendant to pay the settlement "over a very long period" and "in moderate installments." Both parties were happy with the result and Gandhi realized "that the true function of a lawyer was to unite parties riven asunder." (A II, xiv)

His work complete, Gandhi prepared to return to India. His friends arranged an all-day farewell party in his honor. At the party he read a newspaper article on "Indian Franchise." He realized that the article was about a bill that would strike at the root of the self-respect of Indians in South Africa. Those at the party persuaded him not to go but to stay and to fight the bill. "The farewell party was thus turned into a working committee" that "laid the foundations of my life in South Africa and sowed the seed of the fight for national self-respect." (A II, xvi)

The sudden reversal at the farewell party illustrates Gandhi's flexibility and his responsiveness to situations. It was his responsiveness

2

to ideas that motivated him to found his first intentional community. He read Ruskin's *Unto This Last* and shortly afterwards founded the Phoenix Settlement at New Durban.

In addition to his willingness to respond to situations and to ideas, Gandhi's industriousness is also striking. One piece of evidence of his industriousness, accessible in many university libraries, is his *Collected Works*. Although not complete, the collection is ninety volumes and reveals that Gandhi was a prolific correspondent in addition to writing for several newspapers and journals. Ninety volumes would be a challenge for someone today with a word processor, but until he began to dictate to a secretary, Gandhi wrote everything in the volumes by hand except the interviews and some speeches.

The question arises of how someone could do so much. In addition to writing, he gave speeches and interviews, organized campaigns, served time in jail, spun yarn daily, led prayer meetings, spent time in discussions, resolved disputes, responded to critics, and treated the sick. Gandhi attributes part of his energy to his sublimation of sexual energy through *brahmacharya* (voluntary celibacy). Another part of any answer is that, at least after he got over his self-confessed cowardice and shyness, he was no longer self-conscious and uncertain. "Without elaborate scheme I have simply tried in my own way to apply the eternal principles of truth and non-violence to our daily life and problems. Like a child I did whatever occurred to me on the spur of the moment during the course of events." (CW 62, 224) He acted, wrote and said what he thought without worrying about consistency. "At the time of writing I never think of what I have said before. My aim is not to be consistent with my previous statements on a given question, but to be consistent with truth as it may present itself to me at a given moment.... [and has] saved my memory an undue strain." (CW 70, 203) In acting and writing in this way he lived out his favorite ethical text, the *Bhagavad Gita*, which teaches us to do our duty without any attachment to the consequences. That means, in part, without any attachment to whether we will look foolish, or reap praise, or what kind of impression we will make. Someone who lacks attachment in these ways does not use up energy unnecessarily and can better focus on any task at hand.

The task at hand for Gandhi in South Africa was gaining rights for Indians as citizens of the British Empire. That task took twenty-four years. In India the task became one of trying to free India from all forms of exploitation and domination, including colonial rule by the British.

Gandhi was gravely disappointed with the results of that struggle. When the British did leave, they left behind a partitioned India: Pakistan for Muslims and the rest of India for Hindus. The erupting violence between Muslims and Hindus at the end of British rule hurt Gandhi deeply. He fasted because of the violence and his fasts helped avert even more violence. Despite the disapproval of friends and colleagues, he planned to go to Pakistan to try to mend the breach of partition and heal wounds. He never went. On January 30th, 1948, Gandhi was walking through a garden in New Delhi to conduct a prayer meeting. A young Hindu man pushed his nurse Manu Gandhi aside, planted himself in front of the Mahatma and fired three shots at point-blank range. "The last words Gandhiji uttered were 'Hey Ram'," Manu Gandhi reported. "The hands which had been raised in *namaskar* to the gathering slowly came down. The limp body softly sank to the ground." (CW 90, 536) Gandhi was dead.

The violence between Muslims and Hindus ceased. Leaders and spokespersons from around the world praised the Mahatma. "Generations to come, it may be," wrote Albert Einstein, "will scarce believe that such a one as this ever in flesh and blood walked upon the earth." Yet he did, beginning with ordinary insecurities and ineptitudes, much like any of us. Through diligence, reflection, and a willingness to respond to ideals and pressing social needs, he changed both himself and the world in which he lived. He wasn't *born* a moral exemplar or a Mahatma. He *became* what he was through hard work, the confidence to examine conventions and orthodoxies, a willingness to experiment with truth and life, and a responsiveness to events and to ideas.

Gandhi's worldwide reputation suggests that he was successful. We all credit him as the Father of the Indian Nation and the person who led the struggle that forced England to leave India. Yet that was not his primary aim. Gandhi had worked for an India that would not mimic the industrialism of the West but would, instead, become a nation of small self-reliant villages free of violence, exploitation, and unemployment. He had hoped for an India of self-reliant villages that would become a model for all the world.

But India followed the path of Western industrialism. We might think, therefore, that Gandhi had failed. In an important way, he did not. He discovered and left us a clear blueprint that lays out, with provocative clarity, how to live without violence, exploitation, or ecological degradation.

2

Non-violence and *Satyagraha*

Central to Gandhi's efforts in South Africa and in India was his development and promulgation of non-violence as "*satyagraha*." When Gandhi began experimenting with the power of non-violence, he first used the phrase "passive resistance" to describe it but that term created confusion.

> When in a meeting of Europeans I found that the term 'passive resistance' was too narrowly construed, that it was supposed to be a weapon of the weak, that it could be characterized by hatred, and that it could finally manifest itself as violence. I had to... explain the real nature of the Indian movement. It was clear that a new word must be coined. (A IV, xxvi)

Gandhi wrote that, "for the life of me," he could not think of a new name, and so he held a contest through one of the journals with which he was associated. The result was the name "*satyagraha*," meaning truth (sat) and firmness or force (agraha). *Satyagraha* is much more than passive resistance. First, it is not passive. Rather, it is an active but non-violent resistance. Second, the *Satyagrahi*'s non-violence or *ahimsa* extends well beyond the external restraint of violent behavior:

> Not to hurt any living thing is no doubt a part of *ahimsa*. But it is its least expression. The principle of *ahimsa* is hurt by every evil thought, by undue haste, by lying, by hatred, by wishing ill to anybody. (CW 44, 58)

In the West we tend to think of non-violence only in terms of external restraint. Clearly Gandhi includes much more in non-violence. Because it is a method of transformation, it also excludes hatred and ill-will.

Non-violence as a Method of Transformation

For Gandhi, non-violence is to be used as a method of social transformation and as a method for transforming one's "wrongdoers." For this reason,

> It is never the intention of a *satyagrahi* to embarrass the wrongdoer. The appeal is never to his fear; it is, must be, always to his heart. The *satyagrahi*'s object is to convert, not to coerce, the wrongdoers. He should avoid artificiality in all his doings. He acts naturally from an inward conviction. (CW 69, 69)

Although Gandhi was able to provide good reasons to the British for leaving India, he knew that appealing to reason typically did not persuade anyone to change.

> I have come to this fundamental conclusion that if you want something really important to be done, you must not merely satisfy the reason, you must move the heart also. The appeal of reason is more to the head, but the penetration of the heart comes from suffering. It opens up the inner understanding in man. (CW 48, 189)

The suffering he mentions was not to be borne by those whose viewpoints and actions the *Satyagrahi* wished to change. It was to be borne by those seeking change. "*Ahimsa* requires deliberate self-suffering, not a

6

deliberate injuring of the supposed wrong doer." (CW 13, 295) We know from our own experience that if someone attacks us or criticizes us for holding a view or acting in a certain way, our typical reaction is to defend ourselves. Since the satyagrahi does not want to make those she is trying to persuade either fearful or defensive, and hence less open to persuasion, she does not hurt, either physically or mentally, those she is trying to change. Instead, Gandhi's idea was that those who want change would bear the suffering necessary to create the change.

For Gandhi, this was not only the way to behave in a large-scale action against those who would exploit us, but also the way to confront aggressors even in our own homes. Gandhi's example involved thieves:

> We punish thieves, because we think they harass us. They may leave us alone, but they will only transfer their attentions to another victim. This other victim however is also a human being, ourselves in a different form, and so we are caught in a vicious circle. The trouble from thieves continues to increase, as they think it is their business to steal. In the end we see that it is better to endure the thieves than to punish them. The forbearance may even bring them to their senses. By enduring them we realize that thieves are not different from ourselves, they are our brethen, our friends, and may not be punished. But whilst we may bear with the thieves, we may not endure the infliction. That would only induce cowardice. So we realize a further duty. Since we regard the thieves as our kith and kin, they must be made to realize the kinship. And so we must take pains to devise ways and means of winning them over. This is the path of *ahimsa*. It may entail continuous suffering and the cultivating of endless patience. Given these two conditions, the thief is bound in the end to turn away from his evil ways. Thus step by step we learn how to make friends with all the world. (CW 44, 58)

The point is to help the thief see that we are like him and like him we suffer when he steals our things. If we threaten the thief with prison, or with death, of course he may agree not to steal, at least from us. But he is still a thief. Coercion generally does not alter a person's attitudes or habits. "All true change comes from within," Gandhi noted. "Any change brought about by pressure is worthless." (CW 83, 317)

A recent example of a non-violent campaign exemplifying the Gandhian requirement that the *satyagrahi* bears the burden of change occurred in the 1960s during the civil rights demonstrations in the U.S. During some of these demonstrations black men stayed for weeks in Washington, D.C. and wore large signs that said "I am a man." At first glance this might seem puzzling or even humiliating. But these men were bearing the burden of making themselves vulnerable to possible ridicule, or worse, to try to begin to change the perspective of a white establishment that permitted treating blacks as if they were not fully human.

Gandhi's Characterization of Non-violence

Given the non-violent aim of transformation, we are in a better position to catalogue and appreciate both negative and positive requirements of non-violence from Gandhi's perspective. The negative requirements of non-violence or *ahimsa* require "not injuring any living being, whether by body or mind. I may not therefore hurt the person of any wrong doer, or bear any ill will to him and so cause him mental suffering." (CW 13, 295) The positive requirements involve situating non-violence "in the heart and it must be an inseparable part of our very being" (CW 31, 294):

> In its positive form, *ahimsa* means the largest love, the greatest charity. If I am a follower of *ahimsa*, I must love my enemy. I must apply the same rule to the wrong doer who is my enemy or a stranger to me, as I would to my wrong-doing father or son. This active *ahimsa* necessarily includes truth and fearlessness. (CW 13, 295)

Although love is necessary for the practice of Gandhian non-violence, that does not mean that one has to love *what* the other person does. Gandhi distinguished between the *deed* and the *doer* of the deed:

> The doer of the deed, whether good or wicked, always deserves respect or pity as the case may be. "Hate the sin and not the sinner" is a precept which, though easy enough to understand, is rarely practised, and that is why the poison of hatred spreads in the world. (A IV, x)

8

This is an important practical consideration for anyone trying to persuade someone, and Gandhi was clear that we should not vilify opponents:

> Vilification of an opponent there can never be. But this does not exclude a truthful characterization of his acts. An opponent is not always a bad man because he opposes. He may be as honourable as we may claim to be and yet there may be vital differences between him and us. (CW 46, 108)

Rather than hatred and vilification, Gandhi required civility. In his experience with non-violence, Gandhi discovered that civility may be problematic, as he noted in writing about a group of agriculturalists who had rid themselves of fear:

> It seemed well-nigh impossible to make them realize the duty of combining civility with fearlessness. Once they had shed the fear of the officials, how could they be stopped from returning their insults? And yet if they resorted to uncivility it would spoil their *satyagraha*, like a drop of arsenic in milk.... Experience has taught me that civility is the most difficult part of *satyagraha*. Civility does not here mean the mere outward gentleness of speech cultivated for the occasion, but an inborn gentleness and desire to do the opponent good. (A V, xxv)

Without civility, the transformative power of non-violence is lost.

Gandhi thought that non-violence is not only for the dramatic moments when we face thieves or contribute to a social transformation:

> If a person does not observe *ahimsa* in his relations with his neighbours and his associates, he is thousands of miles away from *ahimsa*. A votary of *ahimsa*, therefore, should ask himself every day when retiring: "Did I speak harshly today to any co-worker? ... Did I shirk my duty and throw the burden on my co-worker?... Did I not care even to greet the guest who had arrived?... Did I get angry in the kitchen because the rice was half cooked?" All these are forms of intense violence. If we do not observe *ahimsa* spontaneously in such daily acts, we shall never learn to observe it in other fields and, if at all we seem to observe it, our *ahimsa* will be of little or no value. *Ahimsa* is a

great force which is active every moment of our lives. It is felt in our every action and thought. (CW 50, 96)

Does Non-violence Work?

Gandhi was experimenting with a method that had not, at least in recorded history to that time, been successfully used to free a nation from a colonizing power or to free workers from exploitation. We know more today about the effectiveness of non-violence. It worked in India. It worked in local struggles with the Nazis in Scandinavia, in the civil rights movement in the United States, in persuading the U.S. government to end the Vietnamese War, in the Philippines, in liberating Poland from the U.S.S.R., in bringing down the Berlin Wall, in ending apartheid in South Africa, and most recently in Yugoslavia. Most of this happened only after Gandhi's death, and it is plausible that none of this would have happened without Gandhi's fifty years of promulgating and using non-violence. During Gandhi's lifetime people did not envision non-violence as a viable method of political transformation and he frequently answered objections against it. One objection is that a non-violent practitioner can get herself killed. Gandhi responded:

> Who enjoys the freedom [afterward] when whole divisions of armed soldiers rush into a hailstorm of bullets to be mown down?... But in the case of non-violence, everybody seems to start with the assumption that the non-violent method must be set down as a failure unless he himself at least lives to enjoy the success thereof. This is both illogical and invidious. In *satyagraha* more than in armed warfare, it may be said that we find life by losing it. (CW 72, 234-235)

Another frequently raised objection, then as now, is that non-violence could not work against the Nazis. Gandhi thought otherwise:

> [Non-violent resisters] would offer themselves unarmed as fodder for the aggressor's cannon.... The unexpected spectacle of endless rows upon rows of men and women simply dying rather than surrender to the will of an aggressor must ultimately melt him and his soldiery. (CW 71, 407)

10

Some would reply, citing the atrocities in the death camps and the genocide of the Jewish people, that non-violence would not have worked against Hitler. Yet where people did confront the Nazis with organized non-violence, as in Denmark, they met with success. This hardly proves that non-violence would have worked against Hitler's soldiery, but it does strengthen that possibility. It is important to note that Gandhian non-violence is not a passive resistance that involves people staying in their homes. That kind of *passive* activity has little chance of transforming advancing soldiery. Instead, Gandhi's image is of men and women, without weapons, *actively confronting and not yielding*:

> [Hitler] and his likes have built upon their invariable experience that men yield to force. Unarmed men, women and children offering nonviolent resistance without any bitterness in them will be a novel experience for them. Who can dare say it is not in their nature to respond to the higher and finer forces? They have the same soul that I have. (CW 67, 405)

It is easier psychologically for a soldier to kill people who are trying to kill him than it is to kill unarmed people who are simply in his way. Gandhi's non-violence would have challenged the individual soldiers who would have been required to do the killing. In our arguments and discussions we tend to forget that almost any soldier would rather be back home with family and friends than risking his or her life. If people resist soldiers with awareness and even consideration for their situation, it is not implausible that the soldiers will come to see them as human beings like themselves and will desist.[1] In India during the *satyagrahi* struggle, for example, there were occasions when "opponents threw down their guns and fled--shamed, shaken to their depths by the sign of men who valued the lives of others above their own."[2] In a dramatic refusal to follow orders, the men of the Garhwali Rifles, an Indian unit known for its loyalty, refused a British order to fire on unarmed non-violent demonstrators, saying: "What have they got? They have neither lathis nor stones. On whom should we fire?"[3]

The successful use of non-violence against the Nazis in Denmark involved what Gandhi called "non-cooperation." Gandhi discovered non-cooperation when, during a speech, he needed a plan of action that was broader than a mere boycott. He came up with a plan of action and the word "non-cooperation" to describe it. "The only true resistance to the Government, it therefore seemed to me, was to cease to co-operate with it. Thus I arrived at the word ' non-cooperation.'" (A V, xxxvi) During the speech he did not fully appreciate the potential of non-cooperation but intuitively understand that "it is an inalienable right of the people thus to withhold cooperaton." (A V, xxxvi) Later, Gandhi wrote about the potential of non-cooperation:

> Imagine a whole people unwilling to conform to the laws of the legislature and prepared to suffer the consequences of non-compliance. They will bring the whole legislative and executive machinery to a standstill. The police and the military are of use to coerce minorities however powerful they may be. But no police or military coercion can bend the resolute will of a people who are out for suffering to the uttermost. (CW75, 148)

If a people are willing to bear the burden of suffering, non-cooperation is a viable method for bringing about transformative change.

Conclusion

Non-violence is a method to convert the "wrongdoer" in order to transform a situation into one that lacks the wrongs in question. Since non-violence is meant to be a persuasive tool, it makes sense that among the characteristics of non-violence are respect for the "wrongdoer" and a willingness to bear the burden of change as opposed to inflicting this burden on those whom one is trying to persuade. Although one would expect that those who write about non-violence would take Gandhi's account into consideration, Western theorists typically ignore his account. The few who take it seriously tend to dismiss it. In the next chapter we will examine the orthodox dismissal of Gandhi's challenge to the paradigm of justifiable violence.

----

1. Robert Holmes, "The Sleep of Reason Brings Forth Monsters," *Nonviolence in Theory and Practice* (Belmont CA: Wadsworth, 1990), ed. R. Holmes, 138.

2. Paramahansa Yoganada, *Autobiography of a Yogi* (Los Angeles: Self-Realization Fellowship, 1946), p. 513.

3. D.G. Tendulkar, *Abdul Ghaffar Khan* (Bombay: Gandhi Peace Foundation, 1967), p. 189.

3

Gandhi's Challenge to the Paradigm of Justifiable Violence

Violence has been an integral part of recorded human history and is the paradigmatic way we deal with violence and threats of violence against ourselves and our loved ones. In academic philosophy, self-defense and the defense of loved ones are quick classroom examples of the justified killing of another human being. In discussions of war and revolutions, we typically assume that each can be justified. Both mainstream philosophy and mainstream society condone violence against animals. A majority of people seem still to condone capital punishment, which Nobel Peace Prize winner Desmond Tutu describes as "one of the pinnacle symbols of violence, vengeance and hate in our world today."[1] Overall, people typically accept the paradigm of justifiable violence, as Gandhi noted:

> In this age of the rule of brute force, it is almost impossible for anyone to believe that anyone else could possibly reject the law of the final supremacy of brute force. And so I receive

13

anonymous letters advising me that I must not interfere ... even though popular violence may break out. Others come to me and assuming that secretly I must be plotting violence, inquire when the happy moment for declaring open violence will arrive... Yet others ... have not a shadow of a doubt that I believe in violence just as much as most people do. (CW 18, 131)

Early in his campaign in India Gandhi reported that he had "met practically no one who believes that India can ever become free without resort to violence."[2] Even late in his life he was challenged by people who held the paradigm. "We in the West," said one discussant, "not only believe in violence, but our society is based on it. Several subject races have won their independence through violence and are today living in peace. We have discovered the atom bomb for stopping violence. The last real war is a case in point." (CW 84, 126) Gandhi agreed that Western society was permeated with violence, but did not agree that violence ever brought peace. "It would be absurd to say that violence has ever brought peace to mankind." (CW: 84, 127)

Gandhi's view challenges the orthodox view of justified violence and the two views seem miles apart. Nonetheless, professional philosophers and scholars who have examined Gandhi's writings conclude that Gandhi thought violence was "justifiable," that Gandhi's commitment to violence was "qualified," and that Gandhi's views and ours are in general agreement about justifiable violence. This reading of Gandhi has effectively undermined his challenge to contemporary orthodoxies about violence. In this chapter I focus on this reading of Gandhi's account.

The Orthodox Dismissal of Gandhi's Non-violence

Those who argue that Gandhi thought violence was justifiable refer to Gandhi's preference for violent defense of family over cowardly flight. The following is one passage in which Gandhi expresses this preference:

Some villagers were looted. They had fled, leaving their wives, children and belongings to the mercy of the looters. When I rebuked them for their cowardice in thus neglecting their charge, they shamelessly pleaded non-violence. I publicly denounced their conduct and said that my non-violence fully accommodated violence offered by those who did not feel non-violence and who had in their keeping the honour of their womenfolk and little children. Non-violence is not a cover for cowardice, but it is the supreme virtue of the brave. Exercise of non-violence requires far greater bravery than that of swordsmanship. Cowardice is wholly inconsistent with non-violence. Translation from swordsmanship to non-violence is possible and, at times, even an easy stage. (CW 31, 292)

William Borman argues that, because of Gandhi's preference, Gandhi's position is "a reassertion of a widely-held, commonsense one of a general commitment to non-violence which nevertheless can and ought to be set aside when overriding moral considerations require it."[3] Citing Borman, Virginia Held concludes that "this leaves us with the task of making comparative judgments concerning the use of violence among all those unwilling or unable to adopt 'the summit of bravery', non-violence, and preferring, on the various sides of any given conflict, violence to flight."[4] Robert L. Holmes puts Gandhi in the group of those with a "qualified commitment to nonviolence," a broad group that includes those pacifists who only oppose "war, not all violence," those who "subscribe to nonviolence only because they believe it is effective and do not rule out the use of violence in principle," and still others who view "nonviolence merely as a tactic, to be used in certain specific circumstances and not in others."[5] Jerald Richards claims that, though it is "abundantly clear that the better way, for Gandhi, is always the way of nonviolence," Gandhi also thought that violence was "justifiable," at least if that were the only way we could defend our families from attack.[6]

If these assessments of Gandhi's non-violence were accurate, Gandhi's views would understandably offer no challenge to the contemporary paradigm of justifiable violence. Since most of us are unable to use non-violence in the defense of family, either because we lack the courage or the training, this seems to leave us with the "commonsense" task of deciding when violence is morally justified. The paradigm of justifiable violence remains unscathed. We may return, with our intellectual integrity intact, to the task of determining when violence is justified, as if Gandhi never lived. In what follows I explain why this orthodox dismissal[7] of Gandhi's challenge is mistaken.

Gandhi's Rejection of Cowardice

Gandhi's preference for violence in defense of loved ones, rather than cowardly flight, reflects his view that cowardice makes non-violence impossible, not a view that violence is justifiable. Although many focus on this preference as a justification of violence, Martin Luther King's reading more accurately reflects Gandhi's own view:

> It must be emphasized that nonviolent resistance is not a method for cowards; it does resist. If one uses this method because he is afraid or merely because he lacks the instruments of violence, he is not truly nonviolent. This is why Gandhi often said that if cowardice is the only alternative to violence, it is better to fight. He made this statement conscious of the fact that there is always another alternative: no individual or group need submit to any wrong, nor need they use violence to right the wrong; there is always the way of nonviolent resistance. This is ultimately the way of the strong.... not a method of stagnant passivity.[8]

Gandhi was very clear that, to be non-violent, one has to be brave. "The word 'fear' can have no place in the dictionary of *ahimsa*." (CW 72, 282) As a result, Gandhi was a severe critic of cowardice:

> Non-violence and cowardice are contradictory terms. Non-violence is the greatest virtue, cowardice the greatest vice. Non-violence springs from love, cowardice from hate. (CW 42, 73)

Gandhi believed that a coward could not practice non-violence because the step for the coward is simply too great. It must be emphasized that the concern of the coward is self-preservation. The violence Gandhi prefers in the context is to protect one's family, not to protect one's own person and possessions.

In contrast to the disabling vice of cowardice, the bravery of warriors makes it easy for warriors to make the final step to non-violence. Gandhi experienced this directly when he went to the Northeast Frontier, the territory of the Pathans who were known to be brave and fierce fighters and whose law was: "An eye for an eye and a tooth for a tooth."[9] Although Gandhi's supporters tried to discourage him from going to the frontier, Gandhi told them that he wanted "to teach them [the Pathans] how to fight without violence--how to fight without fear." When he arrived he addressed a crowd of these warriors who had guns slung over their shoulders. "Are you afraid?" he asked. "Why else would you be carrying guns?" Speaking about his own attitudes and his lack of a weapon, he said, "I have no fear, that is why I am unarmed. This is what *ahimsa* means."[10] The Pathans threw away their guns and became the most outstanding of Gandhi's non-violent warriors. Their leader, Abdul Ghaffar Khan, became known as the Frontier Gandhi. All of this illustrates Gandhi's claim that, for the brave, non-violence is an easy step.

To Prefer an Action Is Not to Find It Justifiable

As we have seen, the current orthodoxy is that Gandhi thought violence was justifiable because he preferred violence in certain circumstances. This reading of Gandhi assumes that to prefer one action over another is to imply the preferred action is morally justifiable.

Consider an animal liberationist who believes that we should all be vegetarians because we should not contribute to the unnecessary killing of other sentient beings. This animal liberationist might nonetheless prefer that people eat wild fish rather than factory farm animals because, by changing from eating the flesh of factory farm animals to eating the flesh of wild fish, we are following a well-trodden path to vegetarianism. Encouraging the change to eating wild fish is one approach to try to encourage an omnivore to change to vegetarianism. Because factory farm animals have horrific lives from birth to death and factory farming causes significant environmental harms affecting all sentient beings, eating only wild fish in place of factory farm animals would diminish the suffering otherwise caused to sentient being. Hence, we have an independent obligation, not based on killing, to refrain from eating factory farm animals and so contributing to these harms.

This example illustrates that a person can be committed to the view that a particular activity is not morally justifiable, but nonetheless prefer some instances of this activity in certain circumstances. *Anyone who supports a radical, transformative change or who wants to see the abolition of a harmful and morally suspect practice may come to prefer, in special circumstances, people performing instances of these renounced actions because the preferred actions are part of a*

17

transformative change and because they fulfill other obligations. To fail to hold such preferences might even be condemned as making a fetish of not performing the renounced action and so being counterproductive, at least insofar as one is interested in encouraging people to transform themselves. The logic of preferences within the context of an absolutist system shows that it is possible to hold that an action is to be abandoned while preferring it in special circumstances. This preference is based, in our example, (1) on the fact that the preferred action of eating wild fish is a step closer to what is being promoted (vegetarianism), and (2) on the fact that the preferred action fulfills the additional obligation to cause as little harm as possible to sentient beings.

These two reasons parallel the reasons Gandhi held for preferring violent defense of loved ones over cowardly flight. The first is that being able to act with courage is a character trait that a person needs to develop before she can become a practitioner of non-violence. "A man cannot then practice *ahimsa* and be a coward at the same time," Gandhi wrote. " The practice of *ahimsa* calls forth the greatest courage. It is the most soldierly of a soldier's virtues." (CW 13, 295) Gandhi's preference for violence over cowardice in the defense of family is analogous on this point to the reasoning of vegetarians who might prefer the eating of wild fish to factory farm animals. The animal liberationist who is committed to vegetarianism may prefer people eat wild fish because it is a practical and well-trodden step toward becoming fully vegetarian. In the same way, the advocate of non-violence may prefer, as Gandhi did, that people act courageously rather than cowardly since they would be developing what is necessary for non-violence rather than reinforcing what makes non-violence impossible.[11]

The second reason is that there is a duty to protect one's family. This obligation is analogous to the obligations of the animal liberationist to reduce animal suffering. The animal liberationist, in preferring eating wild fish as a step toward vegetarianism, encourages the elimination of the animal suffering caused by factory farming and the brutality of slaughterhouses. In short, *there is nothing inconsistent with being committed to renouncing a kind of action (eating animal flesh, violence) and yet preferring and even encouraging some instances of it in certain circumstances.*

There is one notable difference between Gandhi's preference for violence in the defense of loved ones and the vegetarian's preference for the eating of wild fish. The vegetarian is preferring a less harmful form of the renounced action to a more harmful form. Gandhi, instead, is preferring a form of violence to an alternative that does not include violence. This disanalogy does not undermine the main point of the analogy. The main point of the analogy is that someone intent on abolishing a kind of activity could, under specific circumstances, encourage instances of that activity because those particular actions typically are a transformative step toward the eventual abolishment of the activity.

Gandhi's preference for courageous violence rather than cowardly flight does not, thereby, undermine the point of the analogy. Violence is still to be shunned and non-violence is to be practiced. It is just that many people will not shun violence, either because they can not or are not yet persuaded, and so it is better for them to perform the courageous action because courage is closer to non-violence than cowardice.

> A non-violent man or woman will and should die without retaliation, anger or malice, in self-defense... This is the highest form of bravery. If an individual or a group of people are unable or unwilling to follow this great law of life... retaliation or resistance unto death is the second best, though a long way off from the first. Cowardice is impotence worse than violence. (CW 85, 281)

Even though Gandhi preferred certain instances of violence over non-violence in these circumstances, he was preferring what is closer to non-violence than the alternative of cowardly flight. His preference, like the vegetarian's preference for people to eat wild fish rather than factory farm animals, is a preference for a transformative step toward the eventual abolition of violence.

Non-violence and Revolution

The orthodox defense of violence against Gandhi's promulgation of non-violence focuses on the case of a violent defense of loved ones as opposed to cowardly flight. When the scope of the potential violence involved large groups of people trying to achieve political or economic ends, Gandhi claimed that non-violence is always preferable. Since the situation in which Gandhi found himself was one of revolution, we begin with his comments on his own aims and techniques.

Gandhi's aims were revolutionary. Not to be under English rule was only a part of the aim. Among the more radical aims was economic equality or what Gandhi referred to as "equal distribution." Gandhi knew that achieving this aim required a structural change in the society:

> The real implication of equal distribution is that each man shall have the wherewithal to supply all his natural needs and no more.... To bring this ideal into being, the entire social order has got to be reconstructed. (CW 72, 399)

Although Gandhi was a revolutionary, he thought that revolutions should be non-violent. He referred to himself as "a non-violent revolutionary." (CW 48, 243) His commitment to non-violence was not based on calculation, but rather on his belief that the means we employ in reaching a goal will also be imbedded in the goal itself:

> They say, "means are after all means." I would say, "means are after all everything." As the means so the end. There is no wall of separation between the means and the end. (CW 24, 396)

Gandhi's insight into the reasoning of means and ends is based on his observations of human behavior. The person not committed to non-violence, he wrote,

> Becomes impatient and wants to kill the so-called enemy. There can be but one result of this. Hatred increases. The defeated party vows vengeance and simply bides its time. The spirit of revenge thus descends from father to son. (CW 14, 64)

Elizabeth Wolgast provides support for Gandhi's belief about the proliferating genealogy of violence. She discusses an example in which a wrong has been committed. To right this wrong, Agamemnon commits an act of violence. But from one perspective his act of violence only creates a new wrong and so, in retaliation, he is murdered. Wolgast continues:

> One might think that now, with Agamemnon's murder, the story has finally come to an end.... It is ironic but now it is

finished. Justice was in the wings throughout, since Agamemnon's dilemmas and his fate are all indirectly determined by what he has done [the original "wrong"].[12]

But the score is not settled, for there are yet other perspectives on what has happened. Enter Agamemnon's children who set out to avenge their father's murder. At no point in this story do we find violence bringing us to a state which does not involve a perspective colored and troubled by the violence that got us there. As Wolgast writes:

> In real life . . . the attempt to get even often works in the opposite direction, against stability and settlement and toward further conflict. This happens whenever the getting even of one side is interpreted as a fresh wrong by the other, and thus provokes a new effort to get even. (Wolgast, 118)

Examples of feuding families, clans, and factions are not uncommon and they tend illustrate Wolgast's point about how a violent means may taint the end toward which we might be striving. Again, Wolgast:

> The problem is not only uncertainty about...the familiar calculations of benefit versus cost. What is problematic is the way the *means affect the coordinates of one's future perspective--ours and others*--how unpredictable these future coordinates are until we regard them in retrospect. (Wolgast, 129; italics mine)

Wolgast has offered a plausible rationale to support Gandhi's claim that we must reject violence if we are trying to create a world that is free of violence. Any act of violence used to try to correct a perceived wrong is typically not seen as a correction by those who bear its brunt. When they retaliate, those who first tried to correct the wrong, or those who share their point of view, see the retaliation as yet another wrong justifying yet more violence. This is how feuds begin and there is no way to end them by delivering a final blow that evens up the score. No party to a feud, or their friends, or their progeny, will perceive the last blow against them as the blow that sets the record straight. Hatred ceases only when we let go of hateful thoughts and attitudes. This, of course, is exactly Gandhi's view and a "new" paradigm: a chance to get out of the ruinous cycle of violence and create a society that is non-violent.

A Standard Violent Example

Gandhi's insight that violence only causes more violence also weighs against the quick classroom example of defending an innocent person with violence. One version of the standard example assumes that the only way to defend an innocent person from an assailant is to shoot the assailant. In this example we are to assume (1) the success of violence and (2) the failure of non-violence. Yet both (1) and (2) are often unrealistic assumptions. Violence not only often fails but is counterproductive (the robber becomes a murderer), while non-violence often works. Gandhi trusted in the power of non-violence and that a non-violent solution would arise when a situation presented itself. If we allow for the failure of a violent defense, which is typically possible in realistic situations, and if we allow for the success of non-violence, which is also typically possible in realistic situations, then this example loses much of its force. In addition, in the example we presuppose that (3) the defender has a loaded gun handy and is trained to use this weapon (or else it becomes more dangerous than helpful). Having loaded guns readily accessible often escalates family arguments, neighborhood disputes, and school hostilities into tragic murders, as well as leads to deadly accidents. But what makes (3) especially problematic is that, as Gandhi would say, once we have set out on this route, it gets away from us. We think that violence is justifiable and prepare for violence, both mentally and physically. We have at this point given up on non-violence. The result is (4): we bypass the range of non-violent approaches, fail to discuss them, and so keep ourselves, both intellectually and imaginatively, in the camp of those who support and defend violence.

This is not to say that Gandhi held the view that violent defense was never justified. Gandhi thought that there were situations in which a violent defense was required. These are primarily cases of defending innocents from attacks by animals. While Gandhi thought that non-violent action could persuade persons, he did not think non-violence would persuade an attacking animal. Gandhi also thought that there may be human assailants who are also beyond the reach of persuasion. Gandhi would not consider a human assailant beyond possible persuasion just because he or she was bitter, angry, jealous, fearful, drunk, driven by ideology, full of hatred, a thug, or a professional soldier, for just such assailants were among those Gandhi and other *satyagrahi*s confronted in India and whom non-violence often persuaded. But if the assailant is a "lunatic" who was furiously "killing anyone who came in his way," Gandhi would agree that it is a duty to use violence against such a "lunatic." (CW 31, 544) The lunatic assailant is as beyond the persuasive power of non-violence as is the nonhuman animal. Except for this very circumspect case, Gandhi held violence is not justifiable against humans even in defense, that we are not to prepare for it, and that it is never to be used to promote social change. In short, Gandhi is promulgating a new paradigm.

Gandhi's Challenge

Gandhi has challenged modernity's paradigm of violence.[13] Gandhi's claim is plausible that we cannot make a radical social change and come out with a non-violent result if we use violence. Even though Gandhi clearly thought that the violent defense of loved ones was preferable to cowardly flight, his preference expressed his awareness that courage is a necessary ingredient in non-violence. But this does not show that violence is justifiable. To prefer an action is not to think that it is justifiable. Gandhi seems to have said as much when he wrote that "even in proved cases of necessity, violence cannot be defended 'on principle.' It may be defended on grounds of expedience." (CW 27, 132)

When we return to the philosophers who initially used Gandhi's preference of courageous violence over cowardly flight to justify their assessment of when violence is justified, Held's discussion is the most illuminating. Her case involves calculating what is at stake in making a transition from a situation in which the rights of members of one group are being violated to a situation in which everyone enjoys an equally effective respect for their rights. Held concludes that "terrorism cannot necessarily be ruled out as unjustifiable" and that "a transition involving a sharing of rights violations... may be less morally unjustifiable than continued acceptance of ongoing rights violations."[14] But *if the goal is a situation in which both groups enjoy effective respect for their rights, it is plausible that violence will not be an effective means to that end.* Gandhi's perspective is plausible: because there is no clear separation between "ends" and "means," violent means will leave us with a result permeated with violence. Gandhi's perspective suggests that we must broaden our discussions and examine more carefully whether we can plausibly use violence to create a non-violent society. In the terms of Held's example, we must ask whether we can plausibly use violence to violate the rights of those in the dominant group in order to create a society in which everyone's rights are effectively respected. King, echoing Gandhi, suggests that we cannot: "The aftermath of nonviolence is the creation of the beloved community, while the aftermath of violence is tragic bitterness."[15]

Conclusion

Gandhi challenged our paradigmatic way of looking at war, revolution, and defense. He was clearly committed to "non-violence" in each of these arenas. Granted, he allowed for exceptions: not in warfare,[16] not in revolution, not for acquiring food or medical information by violence against animals, but as an alternative to cowardly flight in the defense of loved ones. This preference for violence over cowardice in defense of loved ones fails to justify or support violence in the ways assumed by contemporary Western society and contemporary philosophers. Gandhi's challenge to our paradigmatic acceptance of violence demands not dismissal but our attention.

---

1. Rebecca Mahoney, "NH Gov. Vetoes Death-Penalty Repeal," AP, May 19, 2000 [http://dailynews.yahoo.com/h/ap/20000519/us/nh_death_penalty.html].

2. *The Essential Gandhi* (New York: Vintage Books, p. 162), edited by Louis Fischer, p. 118.

3. William Borman's *Gandhi and Non-violence* (Albany: State University of New York Press, 1986), p.253.

4. Virginia Held, "Terrorism, Rights, and Political Goals," in *Violence, Terrorism, and Justice*, ed. R. G. Frey and Christopher W. Morris (Cambridge: Cambridge University Press, 1991), p 78.

5. Robert L. Holmes, *Nonviolence in Theory and Practice* (Belmont CA: Wadsworth, 1990), p. 2.

6. Jerald Richards, in "Gandhi's Qualified Acceptance of Violence, *The Acorn*, Fall, 1995,pp. 11 and 13. Richards raises the orthodox rejection of Gandhi's non-violence discussed in this chapter, and also several objections based on Gandhi's involvement in the Boer War in South Africa and WWI. Gandhi's views toward the British began changing in 1919 (after General Dyer's slaughter of over two hundred peaceful protesters at Amritsar) and continued to change through the 1920's. By the 1930's we find a Gandhi who would not have supported the British war effort, even as a medic. Hence, if we divide Gandhi's comments and thinking on these actions into periods (as we do with other thinkers), we find that the criticisms raised against Gandhi's non-violence based on his involvement in wars in South Africa or in WWI do not apply.

7. In Pam McAllister's *Reweaving the Web of Life* (Philadelphia: New Society Publishers,1982), McAllister says of a series of essays that they "echo Gandhi's statement, 'it is better to resist oppression by violent means than to submit, but it is best of all to resist by nonviolent means'" (p. vi). See also Sergio Cotta, "Nihilistic Signifiance of Violence," in *Justice, Law and Violence*, op. cit., p. 75; and Glyn Richards, *The Philosophy of Gandhi* (New Jersey: Humanities Press, 1991).

8. Martin Luther King Jr., *Stride Toward Freedom* (New York: Harper & Row, 1958), pp. 83-84.

9. This paragraph is based on *Gandhi the Man*, ed. Eknath Easwaran (San Francisco: Glide Publications, 1972), p. 84.

10. Ibid.

11. In his own case, in discussing whether he should participate as a non-combatant in World War I, Gandhi wrote that "I could participlate in the war on the side of the Empire and *thereby acquire the capacity and fitness for resisting the violence of war.*" (A IV, xxxix; italics mine)

12. Elizabeth Wolgast, "Getting Even," in Brady and Garver (Philadelphia: Temple University Press, 1991), p. 118. Hereafter all further references to Wolgast in the next few paragraphs will be to this text.

13. According to Riane Eisler, in *The Chalice and The Blade* (San Francisco: Harper and Row, 1987), the paradigm of non-violence is an older paradigm that began being usurped about 5000 years ago. "The Paleolithic goes back over 30,000 years. The Neolithic age agricultural revolution was over 10,000 years ago.... To these agricultural peoples, enjoying humanity's early peak of evolution, peace and prosperity must have seemed the blessed eternal state for

humankind, the nomads no more than a peripheral novelty. We have nothing to go by but speculation on how these nomadic bands grew in numbers and in ferocity and over what span of time. But by the fifth millennium B.C.E., or about seven thousand years ago, we begin to find evidence of what Mellaart calls a pattern of disruption of the old Neolithic cultures in the Near East" (42-43).

14. Held, op. cit., p. 240.

15. King, op. cit., p. 84.

16. Not at least not after 1919: see note 6 above.

4

Non-violence and Animals

The killing of animals for food, clothing and sport is very much part of our paradigm of violence. Although most of Gandhi's writings about non-violence involved non-violence toward humans, Gandhi took a clear stand on violence toward nonhumans. In the decades following Gandhi's death, human violence toward animals has only grown more terrible, in part because of the advent of factory farms.[1]

Non-violence and Animals

Gandhi was as much against violence toward nonhumans as he was against violence toward humans. Gandhi's underlying view here is that nonhuman animals have the same moral worth as human animals and that any obligations about killing apply equally to human and nonhuman animals. "The same law holds in both cases." (CW 37, 311) A person who held these views would undoubtedly be a vegetarian. Despite briefly experimenting with eating meat when young, Gandhi quickly reaffirmed his vegetarianism and remained a vegetarian for the rest of his life. He held the view that all life was sacred. Yet Gandhi realized that we could not avoid himsa [violence] toward other forms of life:

> We are helpless mortals caught in the conflagration of himsa. The saying that life lives on life has a deep meaning in it. Man cannot for a moment live without consciously or unconsciously committing outward himsa. The very fact of his living--eating, drinking and moving about--necessarily involves some himsa, destruction of life, be it ever so minute. (A III, xxxix)

But this did not imply that we do not have moral constraints against harming other life forms. Unavoidable killing is one thing, but killing that we can avoid is an entirely different matter.

Gandhi thought that it is "our duty to behave toward animals as if life was as dear to them as it is to human beings." (CW 49, 431) Having witnessed the bloody sacrifices of sheep at the Kali temple, Gandhi was stunned at the cruelty. Later a friend told him that the sheep don't feel anything because the drum-beating deadened all pain. Gandhi disagreed. "If the sheep had speech," he said, "they would tell a different tale." He continued, equating the value of human and nonhuman life:

> To my mind the life of a lamb is no less precious than that of a human being. I should be unwilling to take the life of a lamb for the sake of the human body. I hold that, the more helpless a creature, the more entitled it is to protection from the cruelty of man. (A III, xviii)

Gandhi's view, if we take the word 'precious' seriously, is that human and nonhuman animals have equal moral worth. For Gandhi, the view that all animal life is of equal worth imposes obligations:

> The truth is that my ethics not only permit me to claim but require me to own kinship with not merely the ape, but the horse and the sheep, the lion and the leopard, the snake and the scorpion. Not so need these kinsfolk regard themselves [as my kin]. The hard ethics which rule my life, and I hold ought to rule the life of every man and woman, impose this unilateral obligation on us. (CW 31, 101)

28

To the objection that nonhuman animals do not themselves recognize "equal moral worth," Gandhi's reply is that our obligations to them is unilateral. As we have unilateral obligations to protect children, even if the children do not have any sense of obligations toward us, so too, according to Gandhi, we have unilateral obligations toward nonhuman animals.

Although Gandhi held that humans and nonhumans have equal worth, he did not think that we should treat nonhumans and humans in the same way:

> The emphasis laid on the sacredness of subhuman life in Jainism is understandable. But that can never mean that one is to be kind to this life in preference to human life. While writing about the sacredness of such life, I take it that the sacredness of human life has been taken for granted. (CW 84, 231)

Gandhi thought there were situations in which we had to kill a nonhuman to save the life of a human. If we have to choose between allowing an animal to kill a human being under our care or defending the human being by killing the animal, Gandhi thought that we had an obligation to protect the human being. For example, Gandhi thought that he would have an obligation to "kill a serpent threatening to bite a child under my protection, if I could not otherwise turn the reptile away." (CW 32, 72)

Gandhi also thought that we should kill a nonhuman out of compassion to end its agony. Gandhi wrote that he should "kill a serpent writhing in agony, and whose pain I could not relieve otherwise." (CW 32, 72) He also discussed a case in which a maimed calf "lay in agony in the *Ashram*." A physician was called and declared the calf "past help and past hope." Gandhi continued:

> The suffering of the animal was so great that it could not even turn [on] its side without excruciating pain. In these circumstances I felt that *ahimsa*[2] demanded that the agony should be ended by ending life itself. (CW 37, 310)

If Gandhi thought that human and nonhuman life were equally precious, it would seem that he should think it morally permissible to end the life of a suffering human being whose suffering could not be alleviated any other way. Gandhi held just this view:

> Would I apply to human beings the principle I have enunciated in connection with the calf? Would I like it to be applied in my own case? My reply is yes.... In practice however we do not cut short the sufferings of our ailing dear ones by death because as a rule we have always means at our disposal to help them and because they have the capacity to think and decide for themselves. But supposing that in the case of an ailing friend I am unable to render any aid whatever and recovery is out of the question and the patient is lying in an unconscious state in the throes of fearful agony, then I would not see any himsa in putting an end to his suffering by death. (CW 37, 311)

Gandhi clarified the claim that he would feel an obligation to euthanize an ailing human being under the same circumstances that he felt an obligation to euthanize an ailing animal:

> In actual practice such a complete analogy is hardly ever to be found. In the first place the human body... is always easier to manipulate and nurse; secondly man being gifted with the power of speech more often than not is in a position to express his wishes and so the question of taking his life without his consent cannot come with the rule. For I have never suggested that the life of another person can be taken against his will without violating the principle of *ahimsa*. Again, we do not always despair of the life of a person when he is reduced to a comatose state and even when he is past all hope he is not necessarily past all help. More often than not it is both possible and practicable to render service to a human patient till the very end. (CW 37, 410)

Having clarified the practical differences between applying the principle to a human being and to a nonhuman animal, Gandhi wrote that he "would still maintain that the principle enunciated regarding the calf applies equally to man and bird and beast." (CW 37, 410)

Based on these cases, Gandhi concluded: "All have to destroy some life (a) for sustaining their own bodies; (b) for protecting those under their care; or (c) sometimes for the sake of those whose life is taken." (CW 31, 546) The violence in (a) is unavoidable, but we are to try to avoid killing as far as possible and therefore not to eat meat or engage in other practices which require killing. Gandhi thought that (b) is violence but that it is also unavoidable, given our moral obligations. Finally, Gandhi thought that (c) is actually *ahimsa*, based on love and compassion.[3]

A Shift of Paradigm of Justified Killing

While none of this would be especially novel to a contemporary animal liberationist, it does reemphasize the shift of paradigm Gandhi recommended. Gandhi thought that some violence was unavoidable in the process of living, some was required by overriding obligations to humans, and some apparent violence was required in order to end the agony of a dying being whose agony could be relieved in no other way. Nonetheless, as Gandhi summarized his position and compared it with what was then and is now the orthodox position, it is clear that he was recommending a shift in our thinking about violence toward nonhuman animals:

> The West (with the exception of a small school of thought) thinks that it is no sin to kill the lower animals for what it regards to be the benefit of man. It has, therefore, encouraged vivisection. The West does not think it wrong to commit violence of all kinds for the satisfaction of the palate. I do not subscribe to these views. According to Western standard[s], it is no sin, on the contrary it is a merit, to kill animals that are no longer useful. Whereas I recognize limits at every step. (CW 32, 43)[4]

Here is a clear shift in paradigm: violence to nonhuman animals is presumed wrong. This paradigm recognizes a kinship with all animals, while acknowledging an obligation to protect loved ones, an obligation to relieve the agony of our nonhuman kin, and the unavoidable himsa that is involved in our daily actions.[5]

---

1. For a recent book on the abuses on factory farms see Gail Eisnitz, *Slaughterhouse* (Amherst, NY: Prometheus Books, 1997). The classic book on this topic is Peter Singer's *Animal Liberation* (New York: Random House, 1975).

2. The word '*ahimsa*' appears in the original Gujarati version in *Navajivan*, 30-9-28. I substitute it for the word 'humanity' that appears in the English text since I believe it to be a clearer statement of Gandhi's position.

3. To those that thought Gandhi had violated his own commitment to *ahimsa*, he wrote: "Let a man *contrast* the sanctimonious horror that is affected by the so-called votaries of *ahimsa*, at the very idea of killing an ailing animal to cut short its agony[,] *with* their utter apathy and indifference to countless cruelties that are practised on our dumb cattle world. And he will begin to wonder whether he is living in the land of *ahimsa* or in that of conscious or unconscious hypocrisy." (CW 37, 313)

4. Gandhi also adds, what would undoubtedly please the biocentrist: "I regard even the destruction of vegetable life as himsa. It is not the teaching of the West." (CW 32, 43)

5. Gandhi's position is remarkable not only for its internal consistency, but because of his emphasis on the relevance of informed consent in euthanasia. The widespread interest by Western philosophers and lawyers in informed consent was stimulated by the Nuremberg Trials. Gandhi wrote on this topic before the atrocities were committed that were the focus of these trials.

5

Equality
and
Appropriate
Technology

In the previous chapters we have primarily focused on violence as killing. For Gandhi, violence also includes all forms of exploitation and he worked for an India that would be free from *all* forms of violence.

Non-violence and Equality

Gandhi was not just trying to rid India of the British. He had a much more profound aim in mind. "I am not interested in freeing India merely from the English yoke," he wrote. " I am bent upon freeing India from any yoke whatsoever. I have no desire to exchange king log for king stork." (CW 24, 227)[1]

Gandhi's evaluative aims included a non-exploitive and non-violent way of life as well as the non-violent methods to achieve this way of life. These aims explicitly involved the rejection of economic inequalities:

> Economic equality is the master key to non-violent independence. Working for economic equality means abolishing the eternal conflict between capital and labour. . . . A non-violent system of government is clearly an impossibility so long as the wide gulf between the rich and the hungry millions persists . . . A violent and bloody revolution is a certainty one day unless there is a voluntary abdication of riches and the power which riches give and sharing them for the common good. (CW 75, 158)

One can debate whether a violent revolution is a certainty when there is a wide gulf between rich and poor. Much less controversial is the fact that, wherever there is a wide gulf between rich and poor, we find violence, if only in the guise of an armed police force.

Gandhi's statement about the link between violence and the gap between rich and poor suggests that, for Gandhi, non-violence is more basic and that economic equality was a means to achieve a non-violent society. Yet Gandhi's insistence on equality is also basic.[2] As a result, he insisted that "every man has an equal right to the necessities of life even as birds and beasts have." (CW 45, 339) Although his ideal was equal distribution, he knew it would not be realized and therefore worked for "equitable distribution." (CW 33, 167) He clarified what this means:

> Economic equality of my conception does not mean that everyone will literally have the same amount. It simply means that everybody should have enough for his or her needs.... Everyone must have a balanced diet, a decent house to live in, facilities for the education of one's children and adequate medical relief. (CW 88, 26)

For Gandhi, "the real implication of equal distribution is that each man shall have the wherewithal to supply all his nature needs and no more." (CW 72, 399)

Today we assess countries by looking at their GNP or some other monetary measure. Gandhi offered a different criterion of assessment:

34

In a well-ordered society, the securing of one's livelihood should be and is found to be the easiest thing in the world. Indeed, the test of orderliness in a country is not the number of millionaires it owns, but the absence of starvation among its masses.(CW 13, 312.)

Although he emphasized equality, in practice he knew it was the poor who needed a voice. "I am working for winning *swaraj* for those toiling and unemployed millions who do not get even a square meal a day and have to scratch along with a piece of stale *roti* [a thin Indian bread] and a pinch of salt." (M, 197) He suggested that we keep in mind the poorest when in doubt about what action to take:

Whenever you are in doubt... apply the following test. Recall the face of the poorest and the weakest man whom you may have seen, and ask yourself if the step you contemplate is going to be of any use to him. Will he gain anything by it? Will it restore him to a control over his own life and destiny? In other words, will it lead to *swaraj* for the hungry and spiritually starving millions?[3]

The Rights of Women

Given Gandhi's focus on non-violence, it is hardly surprising that he was horrified by "man's atrocities toward woman." (CW 42, 4) Gandhi was appalled at violence towards women:

Of all the evils for which man has made himself responsible, none is so degrading, so shocking or so brutal as his abuse of the better half of humanity to me, the female sex, not the weaker sex. It is the nobler of the two, for it is even today the embodiment of sacrifice, silent suffering, humility, faith and knowledge. (CW 21, 105)

From Gandhi's perspective, "in a plan of life based on non-violence, woman has as much right to shape her own destiny as man has to shape his." (CW 75, 155)

Part of Gandhi's vision for a free India included women having an equal status with men. "Women shall play their part equally with men in this new, free India." (CW 48, 354) Gandhi was firm in his support of equal rights for women:

> I am uncompromising in the matter of women's rights. In my opinion, she should labour under no legal disability not suffered by men. I should treat the daughters and sons on a footing of perfect equality. (CW 42, 4-5)

Gandhi was also an uncompromising critic of two practices then common in India. He condemned the practice of widows burning themselves to death on the funeral pyres of their deceased husbands. (CW 46, 159) He also spoke out against the scandal of "girl" wives and encouraged a struggle "till every girl feels in herself strength enough to refuse to be married except when she is of full age and to the person about whom she is given the final choice." (CW 31, 480)

Gandhi observed that the non-violent struggle for India's independence "has brought India's women out from their darkness as nothing else could have in such an incredibly short space of time." (CW 75, 155) He frequently wrote accounts of the courage of women satyagrahis. He criticized those Congressmen who "have not felt the call to see that women become equal partners in the fight for *swaraj*." (CW 75, 155) In his pointed way, Gandhi added: "Let Congressmen begin with their own homes" and stop treating their wives as "dolls."[4]

Full Employment and Appropriate Technology

Gandhi saw that full employment was necessary to end economic inequality and to ground a non-violent society. His emphasis on full employment led him to what, today, we call appropriate technology. He was critical of the use of machinery in mass production for two reasons. The first, to which we will return in the next chapter, was that machinery allows the groups which control it to exploit others. The second was that the use of machinery created unemployment. (CW 87, 326) Objecting to "the craze for machinery, not machinery as such," he wrote:

> The craze is for what they call labour-saving machinery. Men go on 'saving labour' till thousands are without work and thrown on the open streets to die of starvation. I want to save time and labour, not for a fraction of mankind, but for all. I want the

concentration of wealth, not in the hands of a few, but in the hands of all. (CW 25, 251)

Gandhi considered large-scale machinery destructive because it created unemployment, although he was not against "simple tools and instruments and such machines as saves individual labour and lightens the burden of the millions of cottages." (CW 31, 13) "My opposition to machinery is much misunderstood. I am not opposed to machinery as such. I am opposed to machinery which displaces labour and leaves it idle." (CW 85, 239-240)

Gandhi's aim was full employment and the dignity of labour. For this reason he was committed to "the emancipation of the individual from factory slavery." (CW 48, 442) Gandhi endorsed what today we would call "appropriate technology," that is, technology that is appropriate to the aim and goals and wherewithal of a people in a place. The aim was "not to produce village articles as cheap as possible; it is to provide the workless villagers with work at a living wage." (CW 61, 250) Given this aim, those technologies and social arrangements that would foster full employment were appropriate, whereas technologies of mass production that left people unemployed were not.[5]

Agriculture and Spinning

The principal village industry at that time was agriculture. Gandhi recommended intensive, small-scale farming, composting, and returning manure to the land--practices that would be essential in order not to degrade ecosystems for future generations. These practices would not suffice to create full employment. Gandhi knew that other village industries, consistent with agriculture, were needed to meet the goals of full employment. Gandhi sought an answer to the question of what would be an industry that would grant full-employment and "help India get rid of the grinding poverty of her masses." (A V, xxxix) Even before he saw a spinning wheel, Gandhi realized that this was the technology that could solve the problem of unemployment. Later, he challenged a number of students:

> Apply your scientific means to finding out what such supplementary occupation can be which will serve the needs of 700,000 villages scattered over a surface 1,900 miles long and

1,500 miles broad, and I assure you, you will come to the same
irresistible conclusion that I have, that nothing but the spinning
wheel can do it. (CW 26, 302-303)

Gandhi thought that everyone should spin and some of the classic
photographs of Gandhi show him spinning. "I can work it whilst I am
carrying on this conversation with you," he said to one reporter, "and am
adding a little to the wealth of the nation." (CW 61, 188)

Gandhi believed that the spinning wheel would not only solve the
problem of unemployment, but that its beneficial economic effects would
radiate throughout the community:

> It is not merely the wages earned by the spinners that are to be
> counted but it is the whole reconstruction that follows in the
> wake of the spinning wheel. The village weaver, the village
> dyer, the village washerman, the village blacksmith, the village
> carpenter, all and many others will then find themselves
> reinstated in their ancient dignity, as is already happening
> wherever the spinning wheel has gained a footing. (CW 33,
> 151)

The spinning wheel played a central role in Gandhi's vision of the
creation of an independent India. He believed it could "restore lost self-
confidence" and "bring a ray of sunshine into the dark and dilapidated
dungeon of the half-starved peasantry." (CW 30, 130) He thought it was
"the only foundation on which satisfactory village life can be constructed.
It is the centre round which alone it is possible to build up village
reorganization." (CW 32, 25) The spinning wheel became the central
symbol on the Indian flag flown by the Indian Congress during the
struggle against the British. Spinning held out the possibility of full
employment, economic self-respect for workers, and community self-
reliance. Nor did Gandhi think that the spinning wheel's task was
limited to India. The principle of creating communities in which
everyone would have work and in which everyone supported everyone
else was a message for the whole world, and Gandhi thought that the
spinning wheel was relevant everywhere.

Communism, Capitalism, and Trusteeship

Gandhi's aim that each person should be able to work and to earn what he or she needs is not dissimilar from the goal of communism. But Gandhi adamantly opposed communism. "In so far as it is based on violence and denial of God, it repels me." (CW 25, 424) Gandhi's opposition to communism did not lead him to embrace capitalism. He was a sharp critic of capitalism because it encouraged the exploitation he found inherent in industrialism. Gandhi was committed to an India in which there would be an "abolition of the capitalist system, but not the abolition of capital and capitalists." (CW 48, 247) He believed that there would always be a need for capital and did not think there need be any clash between capital and labour because each is dependent on the other. Gandhi saw the capitalist as just another human being who needed to be converted by non-violence:

> If I would recognize the fundamental equality, as I must, of the capitalist and the labourer, I must not aim at his destruction. I must strive for his conversion... open his eyes to the wrong he may be doing. (CW 45, 339)

Gandhi argued that any violent approach that removed capitalists would leave society poorer, "for it will lose the gifts of a man who knows how to accumulate wealth." (CW 72, 400) To accommodate the reformed capitalist, he developed the notion of a "trustee," a person who would be left in possession of his or her wealth but as a trustee for the society, not for personal benefit. Gandhi was sanguine enough to know that many wealthy and powerful people would not voluntarily become trustees for the society. In the case of the recalcitrant capitalist he recommended non-violent non-cooperation as the means for the poor "to free themselves by means of non-violence from the crushing inequalities which have brought them to the verge of starvation." (CW 72, 401) Since the wealthy "cannot accumulate wealth without the cooperation of the poor in society" (CW 72, 401), it is up to the poor to stop co-operating with those wealthy who refuse to act as trustees. Although Gandhi preferred the trustee system to one of state ownership, he was willing to accommodate state ownership. (CW 59, 319)

Conclusion

Gandhi's views were, and still are, revolutionary. He wanted a society in which there would be no exploitation and no violence. He was highly critical of the treatment of women and thought women were to be treated as equals to men. He worked for full employment, encouraged those technologies that would generate full employment, and was critical of machinery that caused unemployment. He identified the spinning wheel as the technology that would be the catalyst for full employment and rekindle the impoverished villages. Although he criticized both communism and capitalism, Gandhi opposed eliminating capitalists, but wanted to convert them so that they would become the trustees of capital for all of society.

---

1. Gandhi also warned: "Let us not run the very grave danger of reviving the system under a new garb. The same system administered by brown men instead of white men will work the same havoc as now, if not infinitely greater." (CW, 47, 411)

2. "All men are born equal. All have the same soul as any other." (CW 35, 1)

3. *The Moral and Political Writings of Mahatma Gandhi* (Oxford: Clarendon Press, 1968) edited by Raghavan Iyer, Vol.3, p. 609.

4. Gandhi realized that he had given "a one-sided picture of the helpless state of India's women. I am quite conscious of the fact that in the villeges generally they hold their own with their menfolk and in some respects even rule them. But to the impartial outsider the legal and customary status of women is bad enough throughtout and demands radical alteration." (CW 75, 155)

5. Given that our concerns are at least as ecological as they are labor-focused, today we also use this term to refer to technology that furthers ecological values. In Gandhi's time, there was almost no explicit worry about ecological destruction.

6

Self-reliance
and Independence
Versus Globalization

Although we think of Gandhi as only working for the independence of India, he had in mind much more:

> My ambition is much higher than independence. Through the deliverance of India, I seek to deliver the so-called weaker races of the earth from the crushing heels of Western exploitation. (CW 35, 457)

Gandhi saw mass production and industrialism as the vehicles for this exploitation, and saw the major world powers in Europe and America using these vehicles "to exploit the so-called weaker or unorganized races of the world." (CW 48, 164) What Gandhi meant by 'mass production' and 'industrialism' we now call globalization.

Globalization

Currently our two main concerns about globalization focus on (1) global environmental crises and (2) the exploitation of those who are not affluent. Neither Gandhi nor anyone in his time focused on global environmental problems. Nonetheless, in Gandhi's warning about the spread of industrialism he used a metaphor that we would use today to express our concern for the ecological destruction caused by globalization and the consumption inherent in it:

> God forbid that India should ever take to industrialism after the manner of the West. If an entire nation of 300 millions took to similar economic exploitation, it would strip the world bare like locusts. (CW 38, 243)

Today the United States is the per capita leader in consumption of resources. Eco-economist Herman Daly echoes Gandhi's concern when he warns against globalizing U.S. levels of consumption: "Crises of depletion, pollution, and ecological breakdown would be the immediate consequences of generalizing US resource consumption standards to the whole world."[1] Gandhi believed that globalization increases consumption and that through unnecessary consumption we harm others:

> God never creates more than what is strictly needed for the moment, with the result that if anyone appropriates more than he really needs, he reduces his neighbour to destitution. The starvation of people in several parts of the world is due to many of us seizing very much more than they need. We may utilize the gifts of nature just as we choose, but in her books the debits are always equal to the credits. (M, 144)

While overconsumption can cause shortages that can cause starvation, the causes of starvation are more varied. Amartya Sen, the 1998 Nobel Prize winner in economics, has shown that starvation may occur in a country like India even when the supply of food in the country is sufficient to feed everyone.[2] The problem is not always the lack of food, as Sen shows, but can be the inability of the poorest to have access to food. This is not to deny that overconsumption can itself lead to a scarcity of food, but only to acknowledge that factors other than

42

overconsumption also lead to starvation. Gandhi acknowledged one of these factors when he noted that administrative corruption can keep food from finding its way to the masses of hungry people. (CW 83, 270)

The other great concern we have today about globalization is the resultant exploitation of those who are not affluent. Gandhi's focus was on the exploitation inherent in globalization:

> Industrialism is, I am afraid, going to be a curse for mankind. Exploitation of one nation by another cannot go on for all time. Industrialism depends entirely on your capacity to exploit, on foreign markets being open to you, and on the absence of competition. (CW 48, 224)

Gandhi's specific concern was that globalization undermined the rural self-reliant economy and lead to "passive or active exploitation of the villagers as the problems of competition and marketing come in." (M, 244)

Globalization Undermines Self-Reliance[3]

Gandhi saw globalization undermining self-reliance and, thereby, independence. Ladakh is a perfect case study of this process. Ladakh, situated in the Himalayas, was a country in which the people grew their own food, made their own clothing, built their own houses, and did not rely on the global economy for any of its needs except salt. In Ladakh there was no unemployment, no poverty, no homelessness, no overpopulation, and cooperation among people was culturally embedded. People helped each other build homes and harvest crops without exchanging money. Ladakh so thoroughly seemed to exemplify Gandhi's values that one of Gandhi's contemporaries, Martin L. Gompertz, wrote in 1928 that Gandhi would have found in Ladakh "nearly all his heart craves, and each time I get to Ladakh I become more of a Gandhi-ite in my leanings to his utterly impracticable ideas of a world reformed."[4]

Ladakh is also a clear illustration of the effects of globalization. In the 1980s development programs began to bring Ladakh into the global economy. Today Ladakh is amok with consumer goods and has become an importer of both food and clothing. Because Ladakhis import food, they have lost control over the relationship between their own labor and the food they can obtain. The price of grain changes due to the vagaries of tariffs, currency markets, and the changing cost of the fuel needed to produce the grain and to transport it over the Himalayas into Ladakh. As a result Ladakhis, who as agriculturalists were the masters of their own food supplies, are now dependent on conditions not under their control. Because in a consumer economy it takes money to buy food, money becomes extremely important. People become preoccupied with money. With the advent of money people hire neighbors to help with building and harvests, the paid helper wanting to be paid as much as possible, and the person hiring help wanting to pay as little as possible. Money undermines the spirit of cooperation between people and weakens both community and relationships. As money becomes central, the gap between rich and poor increases. In traditional Ladakh, accumulation had natural limits, for one could store only so much grain. Since money is stored in banks, accumulation has no natural limit.

An unfortunate consequence of the change from self-reliance is that Ladakhis have come to devalue aspects of their traditional way of life. In 1993 in Leh, the capital of Ladakh, although there were many restaurants, not one served Ladakhi food. The Ladakhis are surprised when you tell them how much you enjoy their healthily boiled foods, and their surprise underscores how, due to the globalization of what is considered of value in affluent nations, they have come to devalue their own cuisine. Similar observations apply for housing. Traditional Ladakhi houses are large and beautiful. Yet due to the values reinforced by consumerism, many Ladakhis have abandoned their traditional housing for small apartments in dismal buildings made out of grey concrete bricks. This change of housing also fractures families, for in old Ladakh people lived with their multigenerational families in spacious homes. The new apartments are designed for the nuclear family.

The undermining of self-confidence and self-reliance began, as we saw, by a reliance on the importation of basic commodities like food and clothing. To insure independence, Gandhi understood that the local production of food and clothing was needed, for when people are dependent on outside forces for their basic needs, they are dependent on market fluctuations and other economic forces beyond their control. He encouraged people to grow what they needed because when they purchased basic crops, prices would be "subject to the fluctuations of the market." (CW 75, p.151) Gandhi believed that "villages cannot retain the freedom they have enjoyed from time immemorial, if they do not control the production of prime necessaries of life" (CW 47, 89) and so he insisted that "every village has to be self-reliant. Things required in a village should be produced in the village itself." (CW 87, 251)

The Independent and Self-Reliant Village

Gandhi's idea of the independent, self-reliant village was "a complete republic, independent of its neighbours for its own vital wants, and yet interdependent for many others [wants] in which dependence is a necessity. Thus every village's first concern will be to grow its own food crops and cotton for its cloth." (CW 76, 308) To support the self-reliant village, Gandhi encouraged urban consumers to purchase village products in order "to give the villages their proper place." (CW, 71, 103) Everyone was to help "revive village industries by using the products thereof in place of things produced in city factories, foreign or indigenous." (CW, 71, 103) Gandhi encouraged people to purchase homespun cloth, even when it was more expensive and cruder than the cloth imported from English mills. What they were doing was not only buying cloth, he reminded them, but "providing workless villagers with work at a living wage." (CW 61, 250)

Critics even today belittle Gandhi's vision of the self-reliant community. One writer, while praising Gandhi as one of the most important people in the 20th century, wrote that Gandhi's "backward, romantic vision of a simple society seems woolly minded."[5] In his own time, Gandhi was criticized for trying to "turn back the clock" and "turn back the course of modern civilization." To one such critic he responded:

> Why am I turning back the course of modern civilization, when I ask the villager to grind his own meal, eat it whole, including the nourishing bran, or when I ask him to turn his sugarcane into *gur* for his own requirements, if not for sale? Am I turning back the course of modern civilization when I ask the villagers not merely to grow raw produce, but to turn it into marketable products and thereby add... to their daily income? (CW 60, 54)

Today we know that eating fresh, unprocessed food containing roughage is much healthier than eating the overly processed white rice and flour products that in colonized areas become a status symbol of wealth and prestige. We also know that, economically, a region is better off if its people export processed raw materials to which their own labor has

45

added value. We might argue that Gandhi was not turning the clock back. He was trying to turn it ahead.

Decentralization

Gandhi's focus on local farm products and self-reliant villages was a focus on decentralized agriculture and the decentralized production of clothing. Gandhi explicitly embraced decentralization:

> If India is to evolve along non-violent lines, it will have to decentralize many things. Centralization cannot be sustained and defended without adequate force. Simple homes from which there is nothing to take away require no policing; the palaces of the rich must have strong guards.... So must huge factories. (CW 71, 56)

Gandhi thought that agriculture could be decentralized for the benefit of all. A nation of farmers can support itself with the farming of small plots. The decentralized method of agriculture is free from the price fluctuations of world markets, provides fresh produce for local consumption, and typically does less ecological damage than industrial farming, which relies on tractors, uses gasoline and diesel, and spews powdered topsoil into the atmosphere. The decentralized production of clothing can be a means to full employment that also reduces the temptation to set up sweat shops.

Decentralization, however, does not allow for the production of many products to which rural agriculturalists have become accustomed. If we are to have water hoses, we need a factory to produce them. Likewise, if we are to have electric wire, trucks, trains, airplanes, electric utilities, computers, or components for solar electricity, we will need centralized facilities. Gandhi would have agreed:

> I detect no incompatibility in the idea of decentralizing, to the greatest extent possible, all industries and crafts, economically profitable in the villages of India, and centralizing or nationalizing the key and vital large industries required for India as a whole. (CW 80, 352)

Gandhi's design for decentralization was that we should decentralize agriculture, the production of cloth and clothing, and whatever else could be a cottage industry while centralizing any necessary industries, utilities, or services that could not be adequately maintained at the village level. Gandhi believed that decentralized production in small villages would solve other important problems too:

> Granting for the moment that machinery may supply all the needs of humanity, still, it would concentrate production in particular areas, so that you would have to go about in a roundabout way to regulate distribution; whereas, if there is production and distribution both in the respective areas where things are required, it is automatically regulated, and there is less chance for fraud, none for speculation.... When production and consumption both become localized, the temptation to speed up production, indefinitely and at any price, disappears. (CW 48, 163-164)

This element of Gandhian thought has powerful ecological implications. When a people produce and consume within the same locality, they avoid the ecological harms of fuel consumption and the emissions of toxic and greenhouse gases caused by transporting products. Furthermore, because each locality would produce what it needs, it would tend not to overproduce, hence using fewer resources and generating less waste and pollution. Finally, a people producing and consuming locally are more likely to experience firsthand the ecological benefits and costs of their economic activities. This provides them with an awareness that can lead them to live in a more ecologically responsible manner.[6]

Gandhi's goal was an independent economy decentralized in rural villages. This economic structure not only supports non-violence and economic equality but, when locally produced goods are also consumed locally, generates an awareness of the ecological impact of the local economy and so enables people to take these ecological impacts into account. Gandhi did not think that India should mimic the economies that were dominant in the West:

> The economic structure of the country will be worthy of our admiration and will endure only if it is in keeping with the conditions in the country. Our wisdom and our culture will be

47

judged from our ability to plan an economy which takes into account the conditions prevailing in the country. (CW 31, 277)

Progress

Gandhi was criticized as "old fashioned," "anti-progress," and "flying in the face of progress." Yet Gandhi wanted progress in a direction that would develop the human spirit, the human soul. "I do want growth, I do want self-determination, I do want freedom," he wrote, "but I want all of these for the soul." (CW 21, 289) He thought that we were mistaken when we took mere accumulation or mere technological sophistication as indicators of progress:

> In so far as we have made the modern materialistic craze our goal, in so far are we going downhill in the path of progress. I hold that economic progress in the sense I have put it [modern materialistic craze] is antagonistic to real progress. (CW 13, 314)

Others, too, have shared Gandhi's appreciation for a kind of progress that would not focus on the pursuit of a productivity and wealth but, instead, focus on improvements that are consistent with the restraint of production and consumption. Herman Daly makes the distinction between growth (Gandhi's "modern materialistic craze") and development (Gandhi's "real progress") in the following way:

> Respect for the dictionary would lead us to reserve the word "growth" for quantitative increase in physical size by assimilation or accretion of materials. "Development" refers to qualitative change, realization of potentialities, transition to a fuller or better state.... It is precisely the recognition that growth in scale ultimately becomes impossible--and already costs more than it is worth--that gives rise to the urgency of the concept of sustainable development. Sustainable development is development without growth in the scale of the economy beyond some point that is within biospheric carrying capacity.[7]

An economy or a society which turned its back on *progress as growth* would still have plenty of room for *progress as development*, as John

Stuart Mill pointed out:

> There would be as much scope as ever for all kinds of mental culture, and moral and social progress; as much room for improving the Art of Living, and much more likelihood of its being improved, when minds ceased to be engrossed by the art of getting on. Even the industrial arts might be as earnestly and as successfully cultivated, with this sole difference, that instead of serving no purpose but the increase of wealth, industrial improvements would produce their legitimate effect, that of abridging labour.[8]

Real progress, according to Mill, allows for all kinds of developments and improvements but does not favor a kneejerk affirmation of material accumulation. Gandhi would have undoubtedly agreed with Mill in this passage. Like Mill, he approved of industrial developments that produced "their legitimate effect, that of abridging labour" and so welcomed those "simple tools and instruments ... as save individual labour and lighten the burden of the millions of cottagers" (CW 31, 13) without producing unemployment.

Economics

Just as Gandhi offered a plausible conception of progress as an alternative to the commonplace conception, so too he offered an alternative standard for measuring the health of an economic system. Currently we measure economic systems in terms of GNP. The difficulty with this is that every financial transaction is considered a positive addition to the GNP. The rationale for this approach is that each person who engages in an economic transfer has seen it as a benefit. But sometimes the GNP approach is counterproductive. For example, if crude oil is spilt, then recovered and reprocessed before being sold, the ecological degradation caused by the oil spill is not a minus from the perspective of GNP. Instead, because the retrieval and reprocessing of the oil requires activities involving economic transactions that do not occur unless there is a spill, the spill becomes a cause of positive additions to the GNP. The externalized costs of pollution do not detract from the GNP. Or consider another example. When a person grows her own vegetables organically, using seeds she saved herself and using homemade compost for fertilizer, nothing is added to the GNP. If instead this person purchased her vegetables in a market and the market purchased the vegetables from a large farm that grew them from purchased seeds, using purchased fertilizers, and then trucked them hundreds of miles, wearing out tires and highways and using fuel, she would be supporting activities that add to the GNP. Yet clearly the person growing her own vegetables has the ability to produce a fresher product, one that is free from chemical fertilizer and chemical pesticides, and one that she can rely upon given her own effort. While the local organic farmer composts and adds organic nutrients to the soil, the large mechanized farmer tends to deplete the soil with chemical fertilizers, creates topsoil loss with the use of large machinery, adds to greenhouse gases by using fuel for tractors and trucks, and adds poisons as pesticides to the food produced. The GNP does not take any of these environmental or health risks into consideration except indirectly when monetary transactions are required to do cleanup or provide medical relief for persons harmed by toxins or other pollutants. Environmental harms and health harms of themselves are external to this method of measurement, are considered externalized costs, and do not detract from the GNP.

The GNP also fails to measure the success of an economy that is not based on the exchange of money, as in traditional Ladakh. Once an economy becomes a money economy, the GNP rises, often substantially. But so can the social and the environmental costs, as in Ladakh.

The problem with the GNP approach is that monetary exchanges become the criterion of what counts for a successful and healthy economy. Gandhi was critical of economic approaches that jettisoned ethical considerations and only used money as the measurement of economic well-being: "An economics that inculcates Mammon worship, and enables the strong to amass wealth at the expense of the weak, is a false and dismal science. It spells death." (M, 264) Gandhi offered a different view of economics. "True economics," he wrote, "stands for social justice, it promotes the good of all equally including the weakest, and is indispensable for decent life." (M, 264)

Although Gandhi's view seems contrary to the current orthodoxies about economics, they are not contrary to the views of some leading contemporary economists. The 1998 Nobel Prize winner in economics, Amartya Sen, holds the view that when we measure the standard of living, we must not look to the accumulation of money but, instead, should look to the degree to which the people in the economy are able to live well, be properly nourished, and take part in the life of the community. Sen thinks that the measure of the living standard is not money, not wealth, not even contentment:

> It is a question of what the person can do or can be and not just a question of their earnings and opulence nor of their being contented. Freedom is the issue, not commodities, not utility as such. It is, rather, that the living standard can be seen as freedom (positive freedom) of particular types, related to material capabilities. It reflects a variety of freedoms of the material kind (such as to be able to live long, to be well nourished, to take part in the life of the community).[9]

Obviously these freedoms, which Sen also refers to as "capabilities" (hence Sen's analysis is referred to as "the capability approach"), do not necessarily require money, but they do require material bases. For example, if one grows one's own food or builds one's own house with the assistance of family and neighbors, as was done in traditional Ladakh, one's standard of living, analyzed on Sen's capability approach, may be as high or higher than the standard of living of a people who have the money to purchase food and to purchase ready-made houses. This perspective is consistent with Gandhi's in that it puts money and Mammon worship in a subsidiary position.

Although Sen's assessment of the standard of living is an economic one, and so focuses on those material goods that have a measurable material basis, he also wants to claim that various psychological conditions are relevant:

> Being psychologically well-adjusted may not be a "material" functioning, but it is hard to claim that achievement is of no intrinsic importance to one's standard of living. In fact, any achievement that is rooted in the life that one oneself leads (or can lead), rather than arising from other objectives, does have a claim to being directly relevant to one's standard of living.[10]

When we not only take the material bases for capabilities (the capabilities to flourish, live in a healthy way, enjoy family and friends) into account as the measure for the standard of living, but also take into account psychological adjustment, the case for the economic health of Gandhi's self-reliant villages is even more striking. For example, in traditional Ladakh, which exemplified Gandhi's vision according to Gandhi contemporary Gompertz, people worked together, cooperated in building homes, helped each other at harvest, and celebrated together in festivals. These people felt they were part of a community and were at home in it. Once globalization set in, much of this was lost.

Conclusion

Gandhi was a severe critic of globalization and of Western "progress" and "economics." He championed decentralization and worked to reestablish the independent, self-reliant community. Although global environmental problems that affect future generations were not discussed in Gandhi's time, Gandhi's message is deeply pertinent to us as we face ecological crises brought on by overproduction and overconsumption. Eco-economist Daly makes this point in terms of current levels of consumption:

> For all 5.4 billion people presently alive to consume resources and absorptive capacities at the same per capita rate as Americans or Europeans is ecologically impossible. Much less is it possible to extend that level of consumption to future generations. Development as it is currently understood on the United States model is only possible for a minority of the world's population over a few generations--that is neither just nor sustainable. The goal of sustainable development ... will be for all people in all generations. This is certainly not achievable by a more finely tuned adjustment to the standard growth model which is largely responsible for having created the present impasse in the first place.[11]

Gandhi too thought that we should do much more than just "finely tune" the growth model. Instead, he thought that we should rebuild local economies and recreate self-reliant communities. When we take into account all the effects of globalization on human societies, on other species, and on future generations, Gandhi may seem, rather than "woolly minded," an acute and farsighted visionary.

52

1. Herman Daly, *Valuing the Earth* (Cambridge: Massachusetts Institute of Technology, 1993), p. 369.

2. Amartya Sen, *Poverty and Famines* (Oxford: Clarendon Press, 1981).

3. The material in this section is based on Helena Norberg-Hodge's *Ancient Futures* (Sierra Club Books, San Francisco: 1991), the documentary with the same title, and my own experiences in Ladakh.

4. Martin L. Gompertz, *Magic Ladakh* (London: Seeley, Service, 1928).

5. *Time*, Vol. 154, No. 27, December 31, 1999, p. 93.

6. It is the Gandhian emphasis on local self-reliance that lead to the Chipko ("tree-hugger") movement in India. Gandhian activists initially organized to solve problems of unemployment but, after the 1970 monsoon rains caused flooding, they came to understand the connection between bad forestry and floods. This new awareness led them to decide to stop a timber harvest and the Chipko movement was born. See Bart Gruzalski, "The Chipko Movement: A Gandhian Approach to Ecological Sustainability and Liberation from Economic Colonization," *Ethical and Political Dilemmas of Modern India*, ed. by Ninian Smart and Shivesh Thakur (London: Macmillan Press, 1993): 100-125.

7. Daly, *Beyond Growth*, op. cit., p. 167.

8. John Stuart Mill, *Principles of Politicl Economy* (London: Routledge & Kegan Paul, 1965), p. 756.

9. "The Living Standard," *Oxford Economic Papers*, Vol. 36, Nov. 1984 Supplement, p.86.

10. Amaryta Sen, *The Standard of Living* (Cambridge: Cambridge University Press, 1987), p. 27.

11. Herman Daly, *Beyond Growth: The Economics of Sustainable Development* (Boston: Beacon Press, 1996), 162-163.

7

Assessing
Gandhi's Blueprint

In this chapter we explore several rationales that support Gandhi's idea of how we should live, as well as a constellation of challenges to his idea. Since living simply and living in self-reliant community are distinct concepts, we begin with living simply.

Why Live Simply . . . ?

For those of us who have more than we need, the most persuasive reason for living simply is the human and ecological harms caused by our consumer lifestyle. Eco-economist Herman Daly reminds us that our economy is contained in a finite system of resources: the earth and the solar energy we receive daily from the sun. As a result:

> Every time we produce a Cadillac we irrevocably destroy an amount of low entropy [convertible energy] that could otherwise be used for producing a plow or a spade. In other words, every time we produce a Cadillac, we do it at the cost of decreasing the number of human lives in the future.[1]

Gandhi was acutely aware of the harm caused by people living in the "modern style" and warned India against adopting it because India's millions "would strip the world bare like locusts." India did adopt the industrial model, and most countries are joining the global economy as quickly as they can. As globalization accelerates, so do extinctions, the thinning of the ozone layer, global warming, and other negative ecological impacts on current and future generations.

The ecological problem inherent in globalization is excessive consumption. Today we refer to our economy, with no negative connotations, as a "consumer economy." The name is apt and may remind some readers of an early video game, PacMan, in which the player used a "joy" stick to move a little yellow circle with a mouth that was continually opening and closing as it ate as many targets as possible. One difference between what we do in our consumer society and what the yellow PacMen did was that the PacMan consumers did not create waste. We do. We not only consume, we generate an enormous amount of waste and environmental contamination.

In December 1992, the Union of Concerned Scientists issued a document entitled *Warning to Humanity*. Signed by a majority of the living Nobel science laureates, this document warned that "if not checked many of our current practices put at risk the future that we wish for human society and the plant and animal kingdoms, and may so alter the living world that it will be unable to sustain life in the manner we know."[2] The practices about which these scientists were concerned have only increased. Worldwide, we are losing topsoil; polluting the air; draining aquifers; contaminating rivers, lakes and oceans; causing extinctions; pumping carcinogens into the environment; thinning the protective ozone layer; increasing the greenhouse gases; and causing worrisome climatic changes. Before people were thinking about many of these issues, Gandhi recognized the short-term thinking involved in the rapid mechanization of agriculture required by increased consumption. Late in his life he was concerned about the practice of depleting soil fertility for quick returns with mechanized farming practices. The degradation of soil fertility and actual loss of soil have escalated significantly since Gandhi's death. If we continue the way we are going, we may not be able to pass on even to the next couple of generations a planet that can support human life nearly as well as it does now.

When we focus on the ecological costs of our ever-expanding global consumerism, we find one plausible rational for beginning to live more simply. For Gandhi, living simply required rejecting the "artificial increases in our wants" and rearranging our lives in order to "refuse to have what millions cannot." (CW 31, 45) Gandhi suggested the appropriate living standard may depend on local conditions when he criticized the multiplication of wants as "out of proportion to our surroundings"and "unwarranted by the general condition of the country." (CW 31, 44) This leaves those who would live more simply with the task of determining what is truly necessary and could be had by everyone. In the United States, for example, those practicing voluntary simplicity try to live at a "(low) level of sufficiency income," come to see "less as more,"[3] and live without much of what most of us take for granted.

Living simply is reasonable for those who want to mitigate the impacts of rampant consumerism. But why *self-reliant community*?

. . . and in Self-Reliant Community?

Self-reliant communities in the contemporary West, or even those that strive for a significant degree of self-reliance, are practically extinct. In the United States, the automobile is ubiquitous, and, because of the automotive lifestyle, we have built infrastructures that force us to rely on vehicles to commute to work and school, and even require many of us to use vehicles for everyday shopping and even for play. The result is a proliferation of gas stations, fast-food restaurants, strip malls, and huge discount stores, all owned by global corporations. We have designed a way of life that pollutes the air, the water, and uses land that otherwise might be left as green space or used for gardens and agriculture. Even small rural towns are firmly enmeshed in the global economy.

If we are to explore the advantages of self-reliant community we need to look at communities that reflect some degree of simplicity, self-reliance, and egalitarianism. In the United States, intentional communities are about as close as we get to the self-reliant community that grows its own food, nurtures the soil, makes clothing for its members, minimizes wastes, and generally avoids the significant ecological harms caused by the motorized transportation of goods and people (including commuting and shopping).

Gandhi established several intentional communities during his lifetime. Like many contemporary intentional self-reliant communities, communal spaces in Gandhian communities replaced multiple living rooms, meeting rooms, kitchens, and dining rooms. Families and individuals sharing communal spaces drastically reduces the consumption of resources as well as encourages the development of an interactive, cooperative community. Consider Twin Oaks, an intentional community in Louisa, Virginia. Each person has his or her room. In the case of a couple who share a bedroom, the other room can be a private space for creativity, invention, meditation, hobbies, or storage. There are public living rooms for every five or six people, shared bathrooms, and small kitchens available to every dozen or so people. Meals are prepared for the entire community three times a day in a central dining area. One can eat privately at a table, or with one or more guests, or eat at tables designated "open" so that anyone can join. Automobiles and trucks are shared. People work in the community, so there is no commuting. Living in this way, Twin Oaks community members consume significantly fewer resources than people living an equivalent lifestyle a few miles away.

The work schedule at Twin Oaks is illuminating. People work six hours a day, six days a week, and the work, often done in the company of others, includes weaving hammocks, making tofu, gardening, and doing various kinds of office work. That may seem like a lot, but the six hour workload also includes cooking, washing dishes, washing clothes, and cleaning communal spaces. The Twin Oaks resident who works her full share has eighteen hours a day for activities *other than* cooking, washing dishes, washing clothes, or commuting.

In addition to ecological and work-related benefits, each person in an intentional community like Twin Oaks knows that she *belongs* to a community. Even the elderly, who are often considered "useless" in the consumer economy, contribute and have a role. Many of us in the industrialized West long for close-knit, face-to-face community. Community differs from those job-related and professionally focused networks in which many of us find ourselves. In networks, people are there for each other when someone wants to talk about a task or the job. Community involves people being there for each other because everyone basically lives together and is "pulling together."

Moving from an individualistic mentality, according to which every home is to be a person's castle and is to contain the whole household "set" of appliances, tools, and entertainment devices, to a communal mentality is a change that most of us would likely not have even considered a decade ago. But the growing urgency of looming ecological crises demand that we begin thinking about changing, in fundamental ways, the way we live. Economist Juliet Schor, describing the growing movement that is "addressing the environmental, cultural, and social effects of the old American dream and trying to devise a new one," remains positive about our abilities to create a new future:

> It can hardly be possible that the dumbing-down of America has proceeded so far that it's either consumerism or nothing. We remain a creative, resourceful, and caring nation. There's still time left to find our way out of the mall.[4]

Reflection, Not Criticism

A reader may think that the rationales for living simply in a self-reliant community constitute a criticism of his or her own way of life. They do not. Rather, they are ideas generated by what we are slowly realizing about the costs of our way of life. Weekly there are new reports about ozone layer depletion, global warming, rising ocean levels, extinctions, and diminishing supplies of potable water. The rationales in support of Gandhi's self-reliant community arise out of an awareness of the serious ecological costs of consumerism and globalization. The following analogy may clarify that these rationales are not criticisms.

Imagine that three astronauts set off in a spacecraft to land on the moon. On day 3 of their flight the spacecraft suffers an explosion. The astronauts and their ground support assess the situation. Any assessment under these circumstances deals in probabilities, not certainties. Now imagine that, based on the assessment, the chief ground support technician recommends an action that will prohibit any attempt to land on the moon. Understandably both the ground support team and the crew will be initially reluctant to take this step. But, given the data, the step must be taken, and so it is. Looking at this imaginary example,[5] nowhere in this sequence of events is there any occasion for blame or criticism. A crisis, unexpected and unforeseen, arises. Reflection is required, and, if possible, action to mitigate the danger. Understandably, since the action requires a significant change in plans, there is a degree of reluctance.

In our situation, likewise, there is no cause for blame or criticism. People abandoned traditional ways and set out on a sea of change and invention. The momentum of the journey has carried us to where we are today: a consumer lifestyle in which each home is to have the full "set" of household goods and is to be the owner's "castle." We are now discovering that consumerism, as well as nuclear family housing, may not allow future generations to continue the journey. As in the spacecraft analogy, there is no criticism for having set out and arrived where we are today. Instead, the rationales for the Gandhian blueprint are reflections on the unfolding crises and on one alternative available to us.

The Concern for Future Generations

Almost anyone reading this book would find Gandhi's simple, self-reliant community model challenging. Some might find it repugnant. Whether challenging or repugnant, an obvious reason for thinking about making fundamental changes in how we live is that the effects of global consumerism are endangering our children, grandchildren, and those who will follow later.

Not everyone believes that this motivation is adequate. Daly describes a meeting in which "the void of purpose" was "glossed over in discussions with the phrase 'for our children.'" He recalls one woman "evidently so annoyed by the sentimentality of this constant and cloying invocation of 'our children' that she took the microphone to say that she had no children, and was she to understand, therefore, that she had no reason to care about the future of God's Creation?"[6]

The answer to the woman and to Daly is straightforward. Many who are concerned about future generations--including "our" children, grandchildren, and great grandchildren--do not have any children. Talk about being concerned about "our" children and grandchildren can be straightforward talk about our concern for those who will come after us. To be overly literal here is to miss what may be the only motivation we can *all* share for beginning to live in a more appropriate way. One way of suggesting this motivation is in the form of a question intended not only for those who have or will have grandchildren, but also for those who will eventually be in the grandparent generation. The question is: "*What are you going to say to your grandchildren when they ask you, 'you saw this coming, what did you do?*'" Recycling will not be the right answer.[7]

The problems we are facing are vast and are global. Whatever metaphysical account is true of us, human beings are typically delighted at births, care for babies, value children, are able to love each other, and are capable of concern for those who will come after us. That is a firm foundation for enough of us to begin to act.

Could Morality Require Sainthood?

Philosopher Peter Singer argued that those who have more than they need should give of their excess to aid those who are suffering and dying from a lack of food, shelter, and medical care.[8] Singer's conclusion was widely criticized as demanding too much. His critics argued that morality does not require us to (a) abandon our personal projects, (b) become boring and uninteresting, (c) become "do-gooders," or (d) become moral saints.[9] Because the potential obligations generated by a concern for future generations would also be significantly demanding, we will address these four objections as if they were aimed at the claim that we have an obligation to live more simply and in community.

(a) To the charge that morality cannot obligate us to abandon personal projects, Kurt Vonnegut's description of modern thinking seems relevant. He claims that we make "acting for the benefit of future generations seem one of many arbitrary games which might be played by narrow enthusiasts--like poker or polo or the bond market, or the writing of science fiction novels."[10] If the scientific data are accurate, by carrying on business-as-usual we are threatening the very possibility of survival for some future human beings. Assuming this is correct, it becomes unclear what projects could be considered *more important* than living in such a way that we do not cause some human beings after us to perish. Those who think that we have some moral responsibility to other species have even more reason to wonder whether acting in ways that avoid threatening future generations is just one more arbitrary project, like collecting stamps or playing the stock market or writing a book.

(b) To the objection that these obligations would require us to become uninteresting or boring, that objection seems implausible when we examine the rural, self-reliant intentional community. On the face of it, living in this way would require more invention, cooperation, and creativity than living out many varieties of lifestyles of the consumer economy. Consider that people who take steps in this direction often live without "grid" electricity, but use the sun and water and wind to produce the electricity they use. Those who live an alternative style may also produce solar hot water, grow much of their own food, dry or can food for later use, and even make clothing. People who live in intentional communities often dress more colorfully than those of us who are part of the consumer society, and typically spend more time singing, dancing,

60

and in discussion. There is much to interest and fulfill human beings outside of the consumer society that, after all, is embryonic in the history of our species. At least some people would likely find this alternative way of life at least as interesting as an urban job and commute.

(c) To the objection that we do not have a moral obligation to be "do-gooders," we need only point out that whatever obligations we might have to restrain from harming future generations by overconsumption is not an obligation to do good. Rather, it is *an obligation to refrain from doing harm*. To use the do-gooder way of talking, we are focusing on a possible obligation to refrain from being a harm-doer. Such obligations are always serious and do not face the objection that they are supererogatory. Furthermore, in the case in question we are comparing the consumption of what is truly unnecessary for human flourishing against the basic survival needs of future generations. Given this comparison, it becomes difficult to claim that we do not have a moral obligation to refrain from our individual and collective overconsumption of these unnecessary goods.

(d) Finally, to the claim that these obligations require us to be saints, it is important to point out that the issue is not sainthood but a minimum of moral decency not to live a lifestyle that contributes to the suffering and death of future human beings (or to the extinction of other species). Those who live in community know that there is plenty of room for the usual assortment of sinners among those living simply. People get angry, speak harshly, tell lies, break promises, fail to carry their share of the workload, and dally in varieties of sexual misconduct. In short, there is nothing about living simply in community that mandates sainthood. If sainthood were required, there would be no alternative.

Although these reflections on the four objections can lead to further questions and discussion, they are adequate to keep open the possibility that we may have a moral obligations to change the way we live.

Is Life Fulfilling in a Self-reliant Community?

The objections in the previous section seem to presuppose at a motivational level that living more simply in community is less fulfilling than living the life of a typical consumer. Is this presupposition true? Although we cannot hope to give any definitive answer to this question, we can make some comparisons between the consumer way of life and the most radical alternative that the Gandhian perspective might suggest:

the rural, self-reliant intentional community. Our question becomes: are we "better off" living our individualistic consumer lives than we would be if we lived more simply in a rural, self-reliant intentional community?

Urban Hustle versus Rural Life

Gandhi thought that we were seriously deceived when we thought that bigger, faster, and more are better. These are the "positive" goals of modern urban civilization, he wrote:

> Whose roadways are traversed by rushing engines, dragging numerous cars crowded with men who know not for the most part what they are after, who are often absentminded, and whose tempers do not improve by being uncomfortably packed like sardines in boxes and finding themselves in the midst of utter strangers who would oust them if they could and whom they would, in their turn, oust similarly. I refer to these things because they are held to be symbolical of material progress. But they add not an atom to our happiness. (M 232)

Gandhi's disciple Mirabehn saw civilization as a "disease," and "modern man... glories in that sickness, calling it progress, enlightenment, knowledge." Reflecting on a trip to Chandani Chowk, a "grand highway and shopping centre," she writes:

> From all sides every sense was wounded. The din of traffic and shouting of harsh voices beat upon the ears, ugly sights of dirt and tawdriness hurt the eyes, and nasty smells invaded the nose. But worst of all, were the faces of the people, reflecting as they did, the blunted senses and hardened minds within. And this is called civilization. To object to it is called 'putting the clock back'.[11]

Mirabehn continues, asking:

> Have their [civilized persons'] ears been so rasped that they no longer detect the singing of the birds, let alone the voice of the Silence? And their noses, do they seek the city smells rather than the pure sweet air of the mountains?[12]

62

For those who live in rural areas, these reflections carry weight. Those accustomed to urban modernity might reply that Gandhi and Mirabehn exaggerated the bad and failed to recognize the basic advances in our modern way of life: better sanitation, for example, and potable water for everyone. Gandhi would have agreed that these are improvements, but he would have countered that these improvements do not require the noise, pollution, and bustle of today's urban centers. Although not everyone would prefer the slower pace of a rural community, it does seem at least plausible that living in this way would be fulfilling for many.

A Heart Lesson From Ladakh

Several years ago I went to Ladakh, a small area of Northern India which was closed to tourists until the late 1970s. Helena Norberg-Hodge had asked me to give a talk to the Ladakhi women's association, a group of traditional Ladakhi women who are struggling to preserve as much of their recently sustainable society as possible. She had asked me to mention, in particular, the underbelly of our society: the unprecedented number of prisons per capita; the homelessness; the unemployment; the crime. During my talk I described this underbelly, and the women, seventy of them dressed in traditional garb, sat in silence. Since I was talking through a translator, I had plenty of time to think about what I was saying. During one wait for the translator to finish I had the intuition that I should tell these women about our everyday life: how we are with our neighbors, with our fellow workers, and with those we meet in stores, that we often put our old folks in homes with other old folk; and that we tend not to live near our parents or children.

When I said that we rarely share meals with our urban neighbors, and often that we do not even know who they are, these seventy women spontaneously shock their heads and uttered "tsk." When I mentioned that we only infrequently spent time in our homes with those with whom we worked daily, the women again uttered a spontaneous "tsk." They couldn't believe we put our old people in houses with other old people. They didn't understand why we would need hospices. When I told them how far away I lived from my parents and that I saw them at least once a year, not only another "tsk" but some became teary eyed. When my wife told them that she saw her adult children who lived thousands of miles away at least once a year, they cried openly.

These women knew the contrast. They had been raised in a simple and self-sufficient society in which the underlying mode of interaction had been co-operation, not competition. They had known a society in which families lived together, in which adults lived among elders and honored them, a society in which people were in contact with the natural flow of the seasons. Their society had been one in which people loved each other while they had their people problems of fighting, anger, adultery, lying, theft–a society of people who were not perfect but were supportive and co-operative. That a group of women accustomed to living in a sustainable culture would express spontaneous disapproval of much of what we take for granted is a provocative reflection on our way of life. That some of us claim to prefer some of this--anonymity from neighbors and co-workers, distance from family, and no hands-on caring for our elderly–points out the level of selfishness and individualism that is conventionally acceptable and to which most of us are not surprised.

Affluent Living

Economist Juliet Schor cites some "hard evidence" that the affluent lifestyle of consumerism is not as fulfilling as the advertisements suggest:

> Many of us feel we're just making it, barely able to stay even. But what's remarkable is that this feeling is not restricted to families of limited income. It's a generalized feeling, one that exists at all levels. Twenty-seven percent of all households making more than $100,000 a year say they cannot afford to buy everything they really need. Nearly 20 percent say they "spend nearly all their income on the basic necessities of life." In the $50,000-100,000 range, 39 percent and one-third feel this way, respectively. Overall, half the population of the richest country in the world say they cannot afford everything they really need. And it's not just the poorer half.[13]

The consumer lifestyle, even in its own terms of consumption, is not fulfilling for many. When we turn to other criteria of satisfaction and fulfillment, the results are even more troubling. Robert Lane points out:

> The evidence on the rising incidence of depression in advanced economies seems to confirm the belief that market solutions to

the deficit of companionship in modern society have failed. Economic growth is unlikely to be a solution, since precisely those countries that have experienced or are currently experiencing rapid economic growth have the highest incidence of depression.[14]

Lane refers to "evidence of the growing incidence of depression in economically advanced democracies" and that today people in some advanced countries are three times more likely to suffer "paralyzing listlessness, dejection and self-depreciation, as well as an overwhelming sense of hopelessness" than those in their grandparents' generation.[15] Living in a self-reliant community would seem a plausible antidote for this loneliness and depression.

For many of us in the consumer society, we not infrequently see children as burdens, involving us in the pursuit of child care and decent schools from kindergarten through university, as well as involving us in transporting teenagers back and forth between social and athletic events. We more frequently see old people as burdens whom we often abandon to their own loneliness or place in homes with other old people. Televisions "babysit" our children, while adults in the United States reportedly watch, on average, several hours of television daily. Our food comes from stores, our water comes out of a tap, our knowledge of nature often comes from educational television. Some of us haven't smelled a clump of earth or walked barefoot in grass or dirt for years. Those of us who have jobs tend to specialize in one occupation year after year, the weather or the season irrelevant to what we do, commuting to our workplaces by car or sharing a bus or subway with virtual strangers. Although many of us feel time-poor as we work as efficiently as possible to achieve some goal or to acquire what we feel we need, it is not clear, even for those of us who are the most successful, that this way of life is especially meaningful or fulfilling.

In contrast to the consumer urban lifestyle, consider again a rural community[16] that does not run on industrial time and is not committed to acquisition, competition, and industrial-style efficiency. The underlying mode of interaction is cooperation, not competition. Each alternative involves learning again to live daily with children, to live among our elders and honor them, and to be with the natural flow of the seasons. In such a community our knowledge of nature, birth and death does not come from theory and is not transmitted through media. For those who think about the meaning of life, it is difficult to see where else that meaning could be better found.

If It's So Good, Why Are People Leaving It?

One might reply that the above comments are just romantic musings having nothing to do with the informed preferences of real human beings. To those who love life in the fast lane, the slow-paced life of our ancestors, or of people who live in rural areas, or in Gandhian-style communities is a bore. From the fast lane perspective, having a lot of time on one's hands is a symptom of not having enough to do. Given the powerful attraction of the consumer life to people across the globe (which is why globalization and urbanization are accelerating), it would appear that most people agree with these judgments.

This is a serious objection to the claim that living simply is as fulfilling, or more fulfilling, than the consumer lifestyle. Do people really prefer money, excitement, physical comfort, new technologies, medical advances, and ease of travel at the cost of pollution, stress, depression, broken communities, extinctions, and larger prisons? The objection is that they do, for they are making just these choices. But choices can fail to express informed preferences. At issue is whether the choice for consumerism rather than a more Gandhian alternative is informed or made only by people who do not know what is at stake.

People in communities that reflect Gandhian values often do choose consumerism. Ladakh is a perfect example. The people of Ladakh are modernizing despite serious social and environmental costs. If the Gandhian model is so good, why are people fleeing it as fast as they can? Examining what has happened in Ladakh will give us a better understanding of their choice and what it shows.

After Ladakh was opened to the West in the 1970s, the first Westerners who tried to get Ladakhis interested in selling their old pots (as collector items in the West) could not get them to sell.[17] They weren't interested in selling. They had no need of money. The Ladakhi Development Commissioner noted in 1981 that "if Ladakh is ever going to be developed we have to figure out how to make these people more greedy. You just can't motivate them otherwise."[18] This, of course, is a backhanded recognition of Gandhi's point that real independence is to be found in self-reliance and contentment. With those possessions outside influences lose their power to exploit. Helena Norberg-Hodge noted:

When I first arrived in Ladakh the absence of greed was striking... people were not particularly interested in sacrificing their leisure or pleasure simply for material gain. In those early years, tourists were perplexed when people refused to sell them things, no matter how much money they offered. Now, after several years of development, making money has become a major preoccupation. New needs have been created.[19]

The Ladakhis were successfully introduced to consumerism. Their needs were "multiplied." Examining their first steps into a consumer economy will help us to appreciate the degree to which the choice was informed.

The self-reliant person does not see how selling a few pots for a lot of money in any way undermines her self-reliance, her closeknit family, her ecologically sound way of watering her garden and building her intergenerational home. She has all of this, all of it is part of an almost unconscious background, and now, in addition, she has some money. Step one is easy. So, too, is step two. Her son will sell a few pigs, buy a motorbike, and work in the new factory in the nearby town. Again, nothing is lost, or nothing is lost that can't be easily recovered, and something is gained. He has a motorbike and an income. Everything else is still there. If something of value is threatened, he can always return to the traditional ways.

Soon others like him want to do the same thing. With money, it makes sense to purchase something different, since nothing needed to be purchased before: new clothes in the Western style and maybe a small apartment so that he only has to commute home on weekends. These initial changes still seem especially innocuous because, if need be, they can be easily reversed ("I'll just quit the job and go back to my four generation home if this is not satisfying"). But as changes are made and become widespread, the self-reliant ways of the closeknit family and community are lost. People have entered the hustle and bustle of globalization. After awhile, the hustle and bustle is all they have.

Based on the above account, there is good reason to think that the Ladakhis who incrementally moved into the money economy did not fully appreciate that they were abandoning a way of life. At each step of the way it was plausible to believe that a return to traditional ways was a viable option. They were simply adding to the life they already had and not abandoning anything.[20] It is plausible that those engulfed in these transitions did not fully understand what was at stake. When the choice for consumerism and urbanization is made by people who do not understand what they are doing, then their choice does not reveal an informed preference and does not provide any evidence that what they chose leads to more fulfillment or happiness or that what they abandoned is not more satisfying and worth reviving. Gandhi faced a similar objection when he urged people to return to making homespun. "We were producing our own kadi when we lost our freedom," a questioner said to him. "How do you connect the wheel with swarag [independence]?" Gandhi's answer was that the choice to abandon homespun was an uninformed choice and that people did not know what they were giving up. "We did not then know the pricelessness of the charkha [spinning wheel]. Now that we know it, we must restore it to its honoured place in our homes." (CW 71, 156)

Did Gandhi Recommend Rural Self-Reliant Community for Everyone?

Throughout this chapter I have focused on Gandhi's proposal for self-reliant community. I have tried to suggest that, especially in light of the ecological crises that seem to confront us, this proposal is both prudent and sensible. Nonetheless, while it is important to note that Gandhi was committed to non-violence and the equality of all sentient beings, neither of these implicitly involves the adoption of the model of rural, self-reliant community way of life. India during Gandhi's life was a nation of over 700,000 rural villages. It was reasonable in India to emphasize the village economy to provide everyone with the opportunity for economic self-respect and the satisfaction of basic needs. But did Gandhi think that rural villages, or their contemporary manifestations, were for everyone in all countries? He did not seem to think so in 1927:

> The Western civilization is urban. Small countries like England or Italy may afford to urbanize their systems. A big country like America with a very sparse population, perhaps cannot do otherwise. But one would think that a big country, with a teeming population [of] an ancient rural tradition which has hitherto answered its purpose, need not, must not, copy the Western model. What is good for one nation situated in one condition is not necessarily good enough for another, differently situated. (CW 41, 220)

This quote emphasizes Gandhi's pragmatic approach. In light of it, we may wonder whether the rural self-reliant community is even relevant to the West. Following Gandhi's pragmatic approach and acknowledging that what is suited to one situation may not be suited to another, we should ask what ways of organizing ourselves would enhance non-violence and economic self-respect for all. How do urban areas compare with rural self-reliant communities on these two criteria?

It is difficult to think of urban areas free of violence. The number of people in cities requires that most people are indifferent to most other people. In urban areas, this indifference, anonymity, and sometimes fear may begin with neighbors and those living on the same street or even in the same building. Gandhi, the following quote suggests, seems to have thought that non-violence in cities would be impossible because of the lack of contact between people:

> Thirty-four years of continuous experience and experimenting in truth and non-violence have convinced me that non-violence cannot be sustained unless it is linked to conscious body-labour and finds expression in our daily contact with our neighbours. (CW 71, 132)

In cities the indifference of people to each other, or even the fear people have of each other, would make non-violence difficult. Violence is explicit in police forces equipped and ready, if necessary, to kill to protect persons and property. When we turn to the criterion of economic self-respect, the economic hierarchies that are part-and-parcel of all major urban areas require that many people, if they are to work at all, must work at jobs which do not encourage self-respect and often do not provide adequately for themselves and their children. It is therefore plausible that the self-reliant community gets higher marks on the criteria of non-violence and economic equality. When we bring current ecological concerns into the assessment, we have a third reason in favor of the rural self-reliant community way of life over that of urban life.

Gandhi himself seems to have given up on the acceptability of cities by the middle of the 1940s:

> [If] India, and through India the world, is to achieve real freedom, then sooner or later we shall have to go and live in villages--in huts, not in palaces. Millions of people can never

live in cities and palaces in comfort and peace. Nor can they do so by killing one another... But for the pair, truth and non-violence, mankind will be doomed. We can have the vision of that truth and non-violence only in the simplicity of the villages. That simplicity resides in the spinning wheel and what is implied by the spinning wheel.... The world seems to be going in the opposite direction. For the matter of that, when the moth approaches its doom it whirls round faster and faster till it is burnt up [by the flame]. It is possible that India will not be able to escape this moth-like circling. It is my duty to try, till my last breath, to save India and through it all the world from such a fate. (CW 81, 319-320)

This passage clearly shows Gandhi giving up on cities as places where people can live without violence or its threat. Gandhi came to consider "the growth of cities as an evil thing, unfortunate for mankind and the world, unfortunate for England and certainly unfortunate for India." (CW 84, 226) Gandhi would admit that his assessment could be mistaken. Nonetheless, if one wants to foster non-violence, economic self-respect, and a world ecologically able to support future generations, Gandhi's model of the rural self-reliant community is a viable option.

Conclusion

Gandhi's alternative is undoubtedly a radical departure from our consumer way of life. To assess the Gandhian alternative as objectively as we can, we need to begin thinking in a different way than the way we have been educated since childhood--for that way of thinking has created the ecological problems unprecedented in the short history of our species on this planet. As Einstein once said, the problems we face are not going to be solved by the kind of thinking that created them.

Admittedly, it seems almost unimaginable that we will create the Gandhian alternative. Gandhi conceded that this ideal would not be completely realized, but argued that this is no diminishment of its worth.

If we continue to work for such a society, it will slowly come into being to such an extent, such that the people can benefit by it. Euclid's line is one without breadth but no one has so far been able to draw it and never will. All the same it is only by keeping the ideal line in mind that we have made progress in geometry. What is true here is true of every ideal. (CW 85, 41)

Gandhi did not think that we needed to wait until some critical mass of people is ready to begin living out the non-violent alternative before we ourselves begin. Whether it is even possible for a whole nation to turn to plain living, he thought, "is a question open to the doubt of a sceptic. The answer is straight and simple. If plain life is worth living, then the attempt is worth making, even though only an individual or a group makes the effort." (CW 85, 206)[21]

Our consumer way of life is supported by violence, explicitly embraces and models violence, while it increases the gap between rich and poor, causes the extinction of other species, and ecologically degrades the planet for current and future generations. Gandhi has offered us the blueprint for a way of life that is non-violent, supports everyone having basic necessities, is embedded in a simplicity that evades the stresses and strains of the rat race, and is ecologically more sound than the consumer life feeding globalization. This blueprint is worthy of serious consideration.

----

1. Herman Daly, *Beyond Growth: The Economics of Sustainable Development*. Boston: Beacon Press, 1996, p.196. The quote is from his mentor, economist Nicholas Georgescu-Roegen.

2. Union of Concerned Scientists, *Warning to Humanity* (Cambridge, MA: December, 1992).

3. Shor, *The Overspent American* (New York: Basic Books, 1998), p. 138.

4. Juliet Schor, op. cit., p. 167.

5. The example based on the Apollo 13 flight taken in April, 1970.

6. Daly, op. cit., p. 20.

7. Of course we should recycle, but, better still, we should stop consuming products that require recycling. *Recycling presupposes continued consumption.*

8. Peter Singer, "Famine, Affluence, and Morality," *Philosophy and Public Affairs* I, no. 3, Spring, 1972; also, *Practical Ethics* (New York: Cambridge University Press, 1993).

9. Susan Wolf, "Moral Saints," in *The Virtues*, ed. Robert B. Kruschwitz and Robert C. Roberts (Belmont; Calif: Wadsworth, 1987); James Fishkin, *The Limits of Morality;* and Bernard Williams, *Ethics and the Limits of Philosophy* (Cambridge: Harvard University Press, 1985) argue against Singer.

10. Kurt Vonnegut, *Galapagos*, p. 78.

11. *Harijan*, September 29, 1946.

12. Ibid.

13. Juliet Schor, op. cit., p. 6.

14. Robert Lane, "The Road Not Taken: Friendship, Consumerism, and Happiness," *Ethics of Consumption*, ed. by David A. Crocker and Toby Linden (Oxford: Rowman and Littlefield Publishers, Inc: 1998), p. 238.

15. Lane, op. cit., p. 219.

16. One might also compare the Ladakhi alternative, and also Plato's "healthy state," *The Republic* (II: 372-375).

17. Helena Norberg-Hodge, *Ancient Futures* (Sierra Club Books, San Francisco: 1991), pp. 141-142.

18. Helena Norberg-Hodge, op. cit., p. 141.

19. Ibid.

20. See Helena Norberg-Hodge, op. cit., pp. 139, 149-150.

21. People around the globe are working to make changes to protect the environment and to live in such a way that future generations will also have the opportunity to flourish. The Pacific Center for Sustainable Living is a new educational organization that has these aims as part of its purpose (see: www.pacificcenterforsustainableliving.org). Twin Oaks is a community over twenty-five years old that clearly models decreased consumption and importantly, especially from a Gandhian perspective, egalitarianism.

8

Action and Inner Work

The idea that each of us has inner work to do is a dead-on-arrival casualty of the orthodoxies of modernity. Yet anyone applying Gandhi's ideas on non-violence and simple living would need to abandon common reactions, attitudes, and emotional patterns. Doing that involves inner work. Because Gandhi's focus on inner work is so out of step with current academic orthodoxy, it may be helpful to read a contemporary environmentalist, Robert Sutherland, making the case for inner work:

> People have to get involved, they have to act. It's not enough just to be entertained by all of this. It's the time in the history of the planet when all people have to start picking up their share and cleaning up the mess of sloppy cultures, mindsets and philosophies that have resulted in this massive destruction of the earth. We need to reinstate spiritual process. Spiritual process in a healthy religion is one that teaches people to be responsible for their emotions. It teaches us to accept pain and suffering rather than running from it. It teaches us to internalize rather than constantly to act in an imperialistic manner. Most of the consumption, the consumption that is destroying our planet, comes from unmet emotional needs. We need to accept responsibility for our emotions, we need to learn to internalize,

we need to learn to be in harmony with ourselves so that we can be at harmony with all other things. It's basically a spiritual message and a spiritual revolution that have to happen and it begins with every individual, it doesn't begin with overturning the big corporations. The corporations... aren't the cause.[1]

Sutherland touches upon several Gandhian themes: the need to be an active participant, the need to reflect on orthodoxies (mindsets) that support business-as-usual, and the need for non-cooperation with institutions that are problematic (the corporations are not the cause, we are, because we keep them in business). What is most relevant for us is Sutherland's claim that we need to do the inner work of dealing directly with our unmet needs and desires.

Gandhi and Inner Work

Gandhi's own understanding of the literature of inner work did not begin until he first read the *Bhagavad Gita* and the Sermon on the Mount while studying in England. When Gandhi read the Sermon on the Mount, he reported that it "went straight to my heart" and reinforced his belief "that renunciation was the highest form of religion." (A I, xx) Gandhi found the emphasis on renunciation in Christ's teachings important enough to highlight a talk before the Muir College Economic Society. His talk was on the question of whether economic progress clashed with real progress. Gandhi told his audience that Christ eloquently answered the question after the rich young man, unable to give up his possessions, sadly walked away: "'Children, how hard it is for them that trust in riches to enter the kingdom of God. It is easier for a camel to go through the eye of a needle than for a rich man to enter into the kingdom of God!'" (CW 13, 313) Gandhi told his audience that "here you have an eternal rule of life stated in the noblest words the English language is capable of producing" and reminded them that "the disciples nodded unbelief as we do even to this day." He explained why he had emphasized Christ's message:

> I should not have laboured my point as I have done, if I did not believe that, in so far as we have made the modern materialistic craze our goal, in so far are we going downhill in the path of

74

progress..... That you cannot serve God and Mammon is an economic truth of the highest value. (CW 13, 314)

As far as Gandhi could tell, Mammon worship was widespread and had become the religion of Europe. "Europe today is only nominally Christian," he wrote. "In realty, it is worshiping Mammon." (M, 231) He was convinced that progress toward independence could really take place only after people gave up Mammon worship "for the cause of the poor." (CW 31, 46) To this end he formulated his golden rule:

> The golden rule to apply... is resolutely to refuse to have what millions cannot have. This ability to refuse will not descend upon us all of a sudden. The first thing is to cultivate the mental attitude that we will not have possessions, or facilities denied to millions, and the next immediate thing is to rearrange our lives as fast as possible in accordance with our mentality. (CW 31, 45)

To apply Gandhi's golden rule requires renunciation. Renunciation is not only a central message of Christ's teachings, it is *the* central teaching in the *Bhagavad Gita*.

The fundamental message of the *Gita* is that we are to do our duty without any attachment to the consequences. Although renunciation is key, there is nothing passive about it. The *Gita* always puts emphasis on the yoga of action:

> You have the right to work, but for the work's sake only. You have no right to the fruits of work. Desire for the fruits of work must never be your motive in working. Never give way to laziness, either. (2.47; 40)[2]

The prescription not to be lazy does not mean that we should not rest when rest is needed or that we should become workaholics. We have obligations to rest, play, and spend time with family and friends. When we are lazy we typically are yielding to attachments, fears, and aversions. The prescription not to be lazy requires that we renounce these so that we can do whatever we should do.

Critics of renunciation argue that not being attached to results leads to passivity and indifference. Gandhi disagreed:

He who is ever brooding over a result, often loses nerve in the performance of duty. He becomes impatient and then gives vent to anger...he jumps from action to action, never remaining faithful to any. He who broods over results is like a man given to the objects of senses; he is ever-distracted, he says good-by to all scruples, everything is right in his estimation and he therefore resorts to means fair and foul to attain his end.[3]

As the *Gita* says:

> Work done with anxiety about results is far inferior to work done without such anxiety, in the calm of self-surrender.... Those who work selfishly for results are miserable. (2.49; 41)

This, of course, is good advice in every field of life, from public speaking and environmental activism to dancing or carrying on a conversation. Although the *Gita* does not tell us what our duties are, generally we know. If I am driving an automobile down the road, I have a duty to drive safely and pay attention to what I am doing. Likewise, if I have promised to wash the dishes, I should wash the dishes. Often a person can choose among a variety of alternatives, each of which is permissible. For example, it may make no difference at all whether I wash the silverware first or last, or whether or not I play the car radio.

But there are atypical situations in which a person will be uncertain what to do. For example, a person may need to make a decision about a career path or about the direction of activities and commitments. In cases where one's duty is not transparent, the *Gita* advises us to be compassionate and work for the welfare of all creatures:[4]

> Who burns with the bliss
> And suffers the sorrow
> Of every creature
> Within his own heart,
> Making his own
> Each bliss and each sorrow:
> Him I hold highest
> Of all the yogis. (6.32; 67)

Since the *Gita* emphasizes compassion, one would expect that it teaches non-violence. The *Gita*, however, is a discussion between Lord Krishna and Arjuna, who is a warrior on a field of battle. Lord Krishna advises Arjuna to do his duty and kill his opponents. How is this consistent both with compassion and with Gandhi's non-violence?

Gandhi understood the *Gita* not to be an historical text but an analogy for the inner battle between good and evil in each of us. There is no need to put a doctrinaire interpretation on this inner battle. For each of us there are undoubtedly ways in which we would like to be better and there are habits or tendencies that we would like to overcome. Gandhi's interpretation of the *Gita* refers to such inner struggles. On this interpretation, Arjuna's field of battle is an analogy for this inner battlefield. It is the struggle between our good and bad tendencies, each as intimate to us as any parent, sibling, lover, or teacher.

Outer Action and Inner Work

Dealing directly with hatred, selfishness or fear requires inner work. In the following, Gandhi focuses on hatred:

> The first step... is the admission and eradication of whatever hatred there is in one's heart. As long as we harbour ill will or suspicion against our neighbour and do not strive to get rid of it, we cannot learn our first lessons in love. (CW 35, 75)

Gandhi mentions first in this "first step" the admission of hatred. One has to acknowledge an inner condition like hatred before one can skillfully work with it. Gandhi next mentions the eradication of hatred. It is crucial to understand that eradication does not imply repression, for when we repress an inner condition it only tends to grow stronger. One does not act it out or repress it but simply lets go of it. It is no longer "my" feeling but just "a" feeling with which I no longer identify. I no longer identify with it through acting on it (one form of identification), or by repressing it (another form, for a person only represses what is hers), but let it be and subside.[5] As Gandhi noted, "every evil subsides and disappears in the sea of a yogi's mind." (CW 32, 145)

This method of inner work typically involves meditation. Gandhi noted that meditation can lead to the highest inner peace. "Emptying the mind of all conscious processes of thought, and filling it with the spirit of God unmanifest, brings one ineffable peace and attunes the soul with the infinite. (CW 83, 379) There are, of course, other methods of inner work. Although Gandhi was familiar with meditation, the method he tended to emphasize was prayer. "Prayer is the broom that sweeps clean our minds," he wrote. "If we stop praying, all the rubbish and cobwebs will accumulate in our minds and make our inner being impure." (CW 87, 360)

Prayer for Gandhi was not merely the repetition, mentally or aloud, of words. The verbal component of prayer was, for Gandhi, not essential:

> Prayer is no mere exercise of words or of the ears, it is no mere repetition of empty formula. Any amount of repetition... is futile if it fails to stir the soul. It is better in prayer to have a heart without words than words without a heart. (CW 42, 41)

Although prayer was central for Gandhi, he did not think that prayer without external action was true devotion:

> Man does not pray to God through speech alone but through thought, word and deed. If any one of these three aspects is missing, there is no devotion.... The devotees of today appear to think that the limits of devotion are reached in the use of beautiful language and hence ceasing to be devotees become mere rakes and corrupt others too. (CW 36, 296)

External work was crucial for Gandhi and went hand in hand with prayer and meditation. "Anybody who tried to cultivate inward purity without doing [external] work," Gandhi warned, "will more likely than not be in danger of falling into a delusion." (CW 36, 296) Gandhi explained that his own political activities had their source in his spiritual aspiration:

> To see the universal and all-pervading Spirit of Truth face to face one must be able to love the meanest creation as oneself. And a man who aspires after that cannot afford to keep out of any field of life. That is why my devotion to Truth has drawn me into the field of politics... those who say that religion has nothing to do with politics do not know what religion means.[6]

Inner Work and Gandhi's Blueprint

Gandhi's blueprint for how we should live lays out a way of life radically different from the way of life in which most of us are enmeshed. Violence is ubiquitous in the United States and in many other parts of the world. Consumerism and overconsumption are rampant in the West. To become non-violent or to live simply would involve working skillfully with attitudes, emotions, and habits.

To practice non-violence, as Gandhi understands it, requires abandoning hatred and ill. As Gandhi wrote, "the principle of *ahimsa* is hurt by every evil thought, by undue haste, by lying, by hatred, by wishing ill to anybody." (CW 44, 56) To practice non-violent resistance requires overcoming fear and developing courage. If a person were to begin living simply, even more inner work would be required, for she would need to overcome the tendency toward the "multiplication of wants" and "their satisfaction." (CW 33, 164) To adopt a way of life different from the dominant model a person would need all the sources of strength that he or she could muster. One of the most important of them would be the person's own inner strength. Another would involve having friends and associates who value living simply. There are also other sources of support. For Gandhi, one of them was the *Gita*:

> I must confess to you that when doubts haunt me, when disappointments stare me in the face, and when I see not one ray of light on the horizon I turn to the *Bhagavad Gita*, and find a verse to comfort me; and I immediately begin to smile in the midst of overwhelming sorrow. My life has been full of external tragedies and if they have not left any visible and indelible effect on me, I owe it to the teachings of the *Bhagavad Gita.*." (CW 27, 435)

Gandhi knew that the *Gita* would captivate others but he did not think that their attraction was a reason for them to disregard their own religion. Instead, he thought they look more deeply into their own spiritual tradition to find what they had found in the *Gita*.

> Proselytization will mean no peace in the world. Religion is a very personal matter. We should, by living the life according to our light, share the best with one another, thus adding to the

79

sum total of the human effort to reach God. Consider whether you are going to accept the practice of mutual toleration or of equality of all religions. My position is that all the great religions are fundamentally equal. We must have the innate respect for other religions as we have for our own. Mind you, not mutual toleration, but equal respect. (CW 64, 19-20)

In all the great religions Gandhi saw the message of renunciation and the need for inner work. Gandhi believed that inner work was required for outer work, and that inner work also required outer work. Each, for Gandhi, is indispensable if we are to contribute to a world free from exploitation, free from violence, and respectful of all life.

---

1. Taped interview with Robert Sutherland, Redway, California, 1992.

2. *Bhagavad-Gita*, trans. By Swami Prabhavananda and Christopher Isherwood (New York: The New American Library, 1951), p. 40. In the text I will refer to the chapter and verse (here, chapter 2 verse 47) in the *Gita*, as well as to the page number in the translation by Swami Prabhavananda and Christopher Isherwood.

3. Mahatma Gandhi, in *Bhagavad-Gita*, op. cit., p. 143.

4. See also *Bhagavad-Gita*: 5.25; 65.

5. This is one way of describing the Middle Way of the Buddha. See Bart Gruzalski, *On the Buddha* (Belmont, CA: Wadsworth, 2000), pp. 15-16.

6. Easwaran, op. cit., p. 60

9

Gandhi's Legacy

Gandhi's legacy begins with the story of his life. Like most of us, he started with ordinary aims and ambitions. His ambition had been to be a successful lawyer and it was because of this that he found himself in South Africa. Trying to solve the problem of racism led him to refine non-violence as a method of social transformation. This, of course, is his best-known legacy to the world, and it is an important one. Non-violence has been successfully used as a technique for social change on numerous occasions since the time of Gandhi, and Gandhi's promulgation of non-violence has significantly contributed to its use.

By the time Gandhi returned to India he had developed most of the ideas he would be putting into practice during the rest of his life. General Dyer's massacre of non-violent men, women and children at Amritsar helped catalyze a final maturation of Gandhi's thought. In South Africa he had begun a struggle to gain for Indians full respect and status as members of the British Empire. In India, after Amritsar, Gandhi realized that the British had to leave.

Gandhi's aims were more ambitious than just getting the British out of India. He wanted to create a non-violent society in which every person had what he or she needed. He championed the poor and the untouchables. He championed the rights of women in an oppressive cultural setting. He championed animal rights with the subtlety of a contemporary analytic philosopher. He foresaw the dangers inherent in globalization and championed decentralization and the self-reliant village. Although he did not foresee that globalization and consumerism would cause ecological degradation endangering future generations, he did see in general terms that an India of consumers would devour the world "like locusts."

Underlying these problems Gandhi saw what he called the "satanic" side of modern economics: a multiplication of wants that undermined local economies and made everyone vulnerable to exploitation. He offered three antidotes to these problems. One was a revival of the inner life and so a direct attack on the alluring attraction of satisfying a multiplicity of wants. He did not proselytize any particular religion or any particular approach to the inner life, but he did think that this work was essential. "The reforms required are more from within than from without," Gandhi wrote. "A perfect constitution super-imposed upon a rotten internal condition will be like a whited sepulchre." (CW 31, 45) The second antidote depends on the first. Once we are no longer controlled by our desires to satisfy the multiplicity of wants generated by consumerism, we can actively practice non-cooperation and, by no longer purchasing unnecessary products, refuse to contribute to ecological degradation. Gandhi's third antidote was the simple, self-reliant community, which he believed could protect its members from much of the exploitation inherent in globalization. Although Gandhi thought that much of modernity was corrupt and driven by "Mammon worship," he did not reject anything that would be helpful and supportive of the renewal of the self-reliant way of life. For example, he was a constant advocate of proper sanitation in the rural villages, although he did not think that proper sanitation required the other accessories of urban modernity.

If we take Gandhi's views seriously, as we have in this volume, we find that he has challenged three central orthodoxies of our consumer society. The first is that he has provided a plausible account of why violence is never justifiable and never, in the long run, efficacious as a mechanism for social or political transformation. Today, non-violence is widely recognized as a viable technique of social and political change and its use continues to spread. During the completion of this book, for example, hundreds of thousands of non-violent protesters in Belgrade persuaded Slobodan Milosevic to resign as president of Yugoslavia after he lost an election he had initially refused to concede.

82

Second, Gandhi challenged the orthodoxies of consumerism and globalization and his criticisms of globalization strike a contemporary chord. People around the globe are becoming more adamant in protesting against the policies of the World Trade Organization (WTO), the World Bank, and the International Monetary Fund. Critics are calling attention to the kind of exploitation that concerned Gandhi. Focusing on what he saw as a solution to the problems inherent in globalization, Gandhi provided reasons for thinking that rural, self-reliant communities are better than urban centers on the criteria of non-violence and an equitable distribution of goods. If we add to these criteria his (and our) concerns about democracy as a viable political system in a world of powerful and influential corporations, the case for the rural, self-reliant community is even stronger. If we also add our concerns about global warming, extinctions, and other ecological problems, we have a powerful argument in favor of radically rethinking our economic system, our infrastructures, and much more, down to our own individual patterns of consumption. Our task is to assess what we must do to pass on to future generations a world moving toward non-violence, toward full employment, and toward zero tolerance for practices that contribute to ecological degradation. In this rethinking, Gandhi's vision of simple living in self-reliant communities is one viable alternative.

Finally, Gandhi has challenged our mesmerization with material possessions and externals by pointing to the need for us to begin working on those fears and wants that feed the current acceleration of environmental and socially destructive institutions. Without this inner work, a transformation to a non-violent society that does not encourage a "multiplication of wants" seems almost impossible. The widespread interest in yoga and meditation points to the fact that the need for inner work also strikes a contemporary chord.

The relevance of Gandhi's thought to our times is not surprising. He foresaw many of the problems we would be facing. He realized that these problems would be drastic and required solutions that would appear overly drastic to many individuals. "Drastic diseases," Gandhi reminded us, "require drastic remedies." (CW 73, 108)

Glossary

Ahimsa	non-violence
Ashram	a spiritual community
Brahmacharya	celibacy; a vow involving celibacy
Charkha	spinning wheel
Himsa	violence
Kadhi	handspun cotton cloth
Lathis	long wooden poles, often iron-tipped
Mahatma	great soul, a title given to Gandhi
Namaskar	a reverential Indian greeting, with hands placed together
Satyagraha	literally, truth-force; more generally, non-violent resistance
Satyagrahi	one who practices *satyagraha*
Swaraj	independence

Index